"This timely book is perfect for every brand or product marketer who wants to fully leverage the Amazon platform—both for sales and brand exposure. Timothy's practical step-by-step advice is simple to follow and put into practice."
—STEVE FISHER, TEAM LEAD, RETAIL MARKETING, LENOVO

"This book should be called the *Ultimate Guide to Amazon* because it's so much more than just advertising. It's really about building your brand on Amazon. Timothy is able to walk someone through how to do this step-by-step. It was easy to follow. I really enjoyed it."
—MICHELLE REED, SENIOR VICE PRESIDENT, PERRY ELLIS INTERNATIONAL

"The world of Amazon Advertising can be very overwhelming to learn, let alone to succeed in. Timothy does a masterful job at covering important aspects of Amazon Advertising and makes it easy to understand how to begin your brand's quest for success on Amazon. Absolutely glad I picked this up!"
—FAHEEM DAYALA, DIRECTOR OF DIGITAL MARKETING, SILVER JEANS CO.

"Invest a couple hours reading Timothy's book and you will expand your toolkit to build a stronger, more profitable business selling on Amazon. Learn how to develop your advertising strategy including product awareness, brand awareness, brand preference, and customer loyalty on and off Amazon."
—JAMES THOMSON, COFOUNDER OF THE PROSPER SHOW

"Timothy and his team live and breathe digital advertising. His book does an amazing job of describing how to grow your brand on Amazon. I plan to make it required reading for all of my future hires."
—ANDREW JACOBS, CEO, JAM PAPER

"I read *Ultimate Guide to Amazon Advertising* with anticipation because Amazon continues to be a dominant force in the ecommerce world, and I knew from Timothy's experience in the industry and success with his own company, ROI Revolution, that it would be a worthwhile read. I was not disappointed, as it is a useful book for everyone—from beginners to experts—and is written in a concise way that is both practical and enjoyable. I would highly recommend it for anyone who wants to start selling on Amazon, or needs to brush up on the latest offerings from Amazon and techniques to succeed."
—Jim Knight, vice president of ecommerce and IT, Spangler Candy

"We sell to and on Amazon in four countries and started advertising on Amazon two-and-a-half years ago. I love how the book is organized: where to start, what to do next, and everything a brand needs to know at the perfect moment. I'm excited to finally have the tools and tips to grow our brand on Amazon."
—Victor Yacaman, ecommerce director, Leonisa

"Timothy Seward will help you understand why advertising on Amazon is crucial to your brand's success and will expertly guide you through the process. Regardless of your experience level with Amazon advertising, this book is filled with helpful strategies, anecdotes, and data that will help inform your advertising plans, grow your business, and transform your brand. We started using ROI Revolution and Timothy's strategies for Amazon advertising and grew our revenue on Amazon by over 150 percent in the first year. If you aren't advertising on Amazon, you need to read this book and start today."
—Matthew Groom, sales account manager, Brondell, Inc.

"*Ultimate Guide to Amazon Advertising* is a must-read for anyone managing a brand. As a successful entrepreneur and visionary thought leader in the digital space, Timothy has written an easy-to-understand and easy-to-implement prescription for your brand's success. Optimizing your brand on the Amazon Advertising platform has never been more critical in today's marketplace. Reading this book will ensure you revenue and profit growth, along with lasting and positive brand equity."
—Patrice Fontaine Nealon, senior lecturer, NC State University

Entrepreneur MAGAZINE'S

ULTIMATE
GUIDE TO

amazon
ADVERTISING

- Access more of Amazon's 310 million active customers
- Build a profitable ad campaign today—from scratch
- Increase sales of your branded products

TIMOTHY P. SEWARD

Entrepreneur Press®

Entrepreneur Press, Publisher
Cover Design: Andrew Welyczko
Production and Composition: Eliot House Productions

This publication is designed to provide accurate and authoritative information in regard to the
subject matter covered. It is sold with the understanding that the publisher is not engaged in
rendering legal, accounting, or other professional services. If legal advice or other expert assistance is
required, the services of a competent professional person should be sought.

Entrepreneur Press® is a registered trademark of Entrepreneur Media, Inc.

Library of Congress Cataloging-in-Publication Data
  Names: Seward, Timothy P., author.
  Title: Ultimate guide to Amazon advertising / by Timothy P. Seward.
  Description: Irvine, California : Entrepreneur Media, Inc., [2019] | Series: Entrepreneur
    Magazine's ultimate
  Identifiers: LCCN 2019000875| ISBN 978-1-59918-638-2 (alk. paper) | ISBN 1-59918-638-1
    (alk. paper)
  Subjects: LCSH: Amazon.com (Firm) | Electronic commerce. | Selling. | Internet advertising. |
    Internet marketing.
  Classification: LCC HF5548.32 .S49 2019 | DDC 659.14/4—dc23
  LC record available at https://lccn.loc.gov/2019000875

Printed in the United States of America

23 22 21 20 19   10 9 8 7 6 5 4 3 2 1

Contents

"I Teach Google Advertising"

For years, that was my answer when my wife's friends or people at the pub, church, or barbecue asked what I did for a living.

For the first five years, the response I received was usually a furrowed brow. It wasn't exactly obvious to them that Google sold "ads." Google's sponsored listings didn't resemble what most people associated with the word "advertising." Most didn't know what "sponsored" meant at all.

I would explain that those links at the top and right side of Google were paid links. "I don't deal with the *free* side of Google," I would say. "The entire English language is for sale. I help people bid on keywords."

It took a long time for folks to grasp that Google's ads were a total game changer. You could skip the long line and go to the front if you could 1) pay to play and 2) build an economic engine to foot the bill.

The punch line is: by the time most people *did* figure out the game, the easy money had been taken off the table. Those who caught on early made easy profits for years.

Now, years later, it's deja vu all over again—this time, with Amazon. Most Amazon vendors and brand owners are still living in "Amazon 1.0" when, in fact, we are now in "Amazon 2.0." Those with strong organic positions may have time to adjust, but . . . *the clock is ticking.*

If you understand the history of Google and Facebook, the writing is already on the wall.

For years, Amazon advertising was Jeff Bezos' red-headed stepchild. The company clearly did not prioritize these ads. Their ad platform was a *dog*.

All that has changed in the last year or two. The race is on. For the first 20 years, Bezos was content to let shareholders tape dollar bills to every shipment. But now Bezos wants a profitable Amazon.

And those profits will be made *from* and *by* brands who have the *whole* economic model figured out . . . not just sellers hawking a widget.

No one knows this better than Timothy Seward. I invited Timothy to teach Google Analytics at one of my seminars in 2006 because he's one of the most astute players in ecommerce. Timothy and team are eminently qualified to teach this game.

The first sub-head in the preface says: "Upending your business model." Timothy does not state this lightly, and neither do I. This is a total revolution in how the game is played. If you wait very long, it will be too late. This change will put tens of thousands of companies out of business. And it will generate brand new fortunes for the agile and courageous.

This is not a book to casually peruse. This is a field manual, strategy guide, and step-by-step game plan. You sit down at your computer, open this book, create a "science experiment," and use this text to read the battle unfolding before you.

Please: Take Timothy's advice with deadly aim. Sharpen your pencil, sharpen your sword, and capture territory. Your brand depends on it.

—Perry Marshall
Entrepreneur, CEO, and Author:
Ultimate Guide to Google AdWords
Ultimate Guide to Facebook Advertising
80/20 Sales & Marketing

Preface

Simple can be harder than complex . . . But it's worth it in the end because once you get there, you can move mountains.

—Steve Jobs, cofounder of Apple Inc. (1955–2011)

For the past four years, my company has been quietly building our Amazon Advertising management service for some of our biggest brand clients. As we've cracked the code of the brand user experience, we've been managing the Amazon opportunity for an increasing number of them. Now, in this book, I'll share our Amazon Advertising blueprint with you. As you'll discover, there are several benefits to learning how to integrate Amazon Advertising into your brand strategy.

For example, you'll learn how to capture strong "first mover" advantage in Amazon top-position listings over your still-sleepy competitors. Got a new product launch? Test, then accelerate the sale of your new products on Amazon first—without expensive, multimedia-fueled national ad campaigns. Finally, with the increased velocity in your sales on Amazon, you'll attract more attention from consumers as well as managers at Amazon.

Whether you want to explore the possibility of getting started as a first-party vendor or a brand seller on the marketplace, or you're a seasoned brand executive wanting to get a feel for your potential for further growth, you've come to the right place to accelerate your brand's momentum.

After reading this book, you will have the context and tools to build an aggressive, streamlined Amazon advertising campaign for your brand that's proven to increase your Amazon search visibility and consistently capture consumer demand in your category. You can start by rethinking your business model.

UPENDING YOUR BUSINESS MODEL

Flipping the script on your old business model can pay big dividends. You can multiply your brand's reach by stepping into a thriving business model that meets the biggest demands of today's consumers in ways you can't easily do on your own.

Here's an example of what that looks like. In the mid-1990s, I was driving west on Interstate 4 near Lakeland, Florida, when I spotted a massive furniture warehouse with an unusual name—Rooms To Go. Earlier that day, I had noticed one of their bright, gleaming retail stores in Orlando. I made a mental note of the company name, and I've been a student of the enterprise and how it has grown ever since.

After I got home that day, I started to find out all I could about the history of this unusual retail store. Here's what I learned: Like every industry, furniture retailers have their own set of entrenched business practices. The heft and customizability of furniture leads to manufacturing and shipping constraints, forcing many consumers to settle for 6- to 12-week delays between order and delivery. Even in this model, Seaman Furniture Company (the parent company of Rooms To Go) was successful enough that they were bought out for $350 million in 1988.

After the dust settled, the founders exited Seaman and upended the business model by opening their first Rooms To Go store in Orlando in September 1990. They shifted from selling individual customized pieces requiring long delays to selling entire rooms of furniture at once delivered the next day. This new concept required enormous operational changes, such as huge warehouses and distribution centers, much like the one I spotted on I-4 some 20 years ago.

They are still at it today. Rooms To Go recently opened a beautiful new distribution center on Interstate 95, about 30 minutes from my company's campus in Raleigh, North Carolina. This massive 1.45-*million*-square-foot building sits on 115 acres of land and follows the same concept with a 65,000-square-foot retail center attached.

Here are the major lessons I've extracted from their story, which can serve as a guide to upend your own business model:

- *They changed the product.* By selling entire rooms instead of individual pieces, it suddenly became easier for customers to decorate their homes without the stress and uncertainty of the traditional a la carte model. Every piece matched, so there was no need for costly, time-consuming customization.

- *They changed the pricing model.* First, they boosted average order value and profit-per-customer by selling "rooms." Because their customers didn't require customized products, Rooms To Go could negotiate much lower wholesale rates on their bulk furniture orders and now even manufactures much of the furniture themselves, which further increases margins.
- *They changed the promise.* A 12-week wait became "get it tomorrow." They essentially got into the instant gratification business—an industry that has tripled sales (and then some) for some ecommerce companies.

In hindsight, I realize one of the reasons I was so fascinated with the Rooms To Go model is that I had earlier discovered the power of instant gratification firsthand when I owned a four-store auto accessory installation retail chain. Over a few years, I grew automotive sunroof sales/installations from 40–50 yearly to 2,000+ yearly once I began promoting a new service promise of "sunroofs installed while you wait, no appointment necessary." In short, my brand made a promise of "simple and fast."

SIMPLE AND FAST

Conceptually, I'm sure you agree with a "simple and fast" model like the one Rooms To Go uses. But you're also probably not about to go buy hundreds of acres of land and build massive distribution centers scattered across the country.

You should always strive to innovate in your own business, but as far as distribution goes, the great news is that a disruptive business model has already been created by Amazon. They've done the hard work to make it simple and fast for consumers. You can piggyback on their model, momentum, and market without a massive investment or a ton of risk.

Of course, in many ways, companies are justified in seeing Amazon as a competitor; by carrying virtually every popular consumer brand on their site, it's a constant threat to your ability to stand apart and maintain your pricing practices. But because 48 percent of all U.S. online retail sales were done through Amazon in 2018, you are sabotaging your brand's growth by not implementing a smart Amazon advertising strategy.

Amazon goes out of their way to make buying simple and delivery fast for their customers, but doing business is not as easy for their vendors and marketplace merchants. It's rather complicated to sell to and on Amazon due to frequently fluctuating prices, scheming competitors, an ever-changing list of product data requirements, and new beta programs. Finally, the site's constantly changing emphasis on Sponsored Products (ads that appear in search results and product pages on Amazon) and Sponsored Brands (ads that appear in search results and feature your brand logo, a customizable headline, and up to three of your products)—formerly known as Headline Search ads—bring search advertising elements into the mix, which further complicate success.

The good news, though, is that Amazon has a strong existing platform you can build your brand on. And this book will give you the tools you need to succeed in marketing your company's strongest products.

YOUR MISSION: OPTIMIZING YOUR BRAND'S GROWTH ON- AND OFFLINE

So what can you do to take advantage of this incredibly strong growth opportunity? Your mission is to leverage the Amazon Advertising console to grow your brand, both online and offline.

While advertising on Amazon can—and does—drive sales consummated on Amazon itself, the influence of the platform extends into physical stores, where most retail buying still occurs.

Imagine that you're in Office Depot one Saturday morning studying a few printer/scanner/copier all-in-one units for your home office. The four-bullet price/feature card is just not giving you the information you're looking for. Where do you go to learn more and read reviews from past buyers? You pull out your phone and go to Amazon, of course! If you love what you learn, you can walk out of the store with product in hand. Even though you purchased the product in person, you still used the power of Amazon to make your decision.

And, of course, your phone is a direct portal to buying on the site, which may affect your in-store buying down the road. A few months ago, I was looking at my (not so clean) black granite countertop island in the kitchen and decided to find something to make it look great. I grabbed my phone and searched Amazon for "granite cleaner wipes," and saw a brand by Weiman in a Sponsored Products ad on the search results page. I immediately bought two containers, and we've been using it (with great results) ever since. Just recently, I noticed the Weiman brand on the shelf at the grocery store where we do most of our shopping. You can bet we'll be dropping it in our shopping cart now when we get low because we've formed a new connection with a brand we like and trust thanks to the purchase I made on Amazon.

For your brand, the obvious takeaway is this: to effectively market your products both online and off, you've got to get your Amazon advertising strategy right. If you treat Amazon exclusively as a channel for online sales, you will seriously stifle your overall marketing plan. I've seen brands allocate 10 to 30 percent of their total digital advertising budget to Amazon. Yes, Amazon is an engine of demand, but don't restrict your view of it to what happens online as a direct result of trackable revenue driven by ads. Its benefits extend much further than that.

Your mission is to read this book, apply what you've learned to grow your brand, leverage Amazon Advertising to acquire new customers, and provide an easy way for customers to find your products, both online and off.

WHO THIS BOOK IS FOR

This book is primarily for the owner, executive, or team member of a brand that makes or sells products that are sold on the Amazon.com website. If your company owns the full trademark rights to the product brand or has the exclusive right to distribute one or more brands' products, I've written this just for you.

Throughout the book, I'll reference the interface difference that (as of press time) exists between brands that sell *to* Amazon (that have a "first party" relationship and access the Amazon ad interface through the Advertising console, formerly known as AMS) and brands that sell *on* Amazon (that have a "third party" relationship, meaning they list their products for sale on the Amazon marketplace, accessed through the Seller Central page), so either way you'll know where to go when building your Amazon ad campaigns.

You can access most of the Advertising offerings once you sign in at https://advertising.amazon.com.

HOW TO USE THIS BOOK

I recommend that both beginners and those with a solid foundation read this book from beginning to end. If there are sections that don't apply to you (for example, if you sell only to Amazon or sell only to consumers via the Amazon marketplace), I'll tell you where to skip ahead.

Once you've read the book from front to back, feel free to reread any section you need more help on.

One additional word about this book. Much is expected to change in the Amazon Advertising interface over the next few years. Really, the moment we locked down our last word for this book in preparation for printing, I knew to expect minor to major changes. There is no way around that with any dynamic online advertising console or platform. So while this is a "how to" book on Amazon Advertising for brands, I've worked hard to also incorporate broader business marketing concepts that will not change. I've included stories (personal, business, and client) to inspire and (hopefully) entertain you while reading.

Finally, I've set up a section of our website where you can get updates to the book as the Amazon Advertising interface changes. Go to https://www.roirevolution.com/amazonadvertising to get immediate access to changes as Amazon updates their ad ecosystem.

Let's jump right in! In our first chapter, I'll introduce you to the concept behind Amazon's role as a product search engine, how Amazon Advertising helps you and Amazon, how to maximize your position in business by growing your own unique brand, and a simple yet viable Amazon strategy for your brand.

Chapter 1

Stacking Your Brand's Deck on Amazon

Free will and determinism, I was told, are like a game of cards.
The hand that is dealt you represents determinism. The way
you play your hand represent[s] free will.

—NORMAN COUSINS, AMERICAN POLITICAL JOURNALIST, AUTHOR,

AND WORLD PEACE ADVOCATE (1915–1990)

Amazon recorded its first noncompany customer sale on April 3, 1995 when John Wainwright, an Australian software engineer (and a friend of Shel Kaphan, Amazon's first employee), purchased *Fluid Concepts and Creative Analogies: Computer Models of the Fundamental Mechanisms of Thought* by Douglas Hofstadter. Within two months, Amazon's book sales were up to $20,000 per week with sales to all 50 states and 45 countries.

Just 23 months after that, on May 15, 1997, Amazon issued its IPO at a price of $18 per share (after three stock splits in the late 1990s, that's the equivalent today of $1.50 per share).

By 2018, 21 years after its IPO, Amazon recorded about $7,385 in revenue per second, or almost $27 million in revenue per hour, as customers around the world purchased an astronomical amount of goods and services from the site. And that means there are huge opportunities for your brand on Amazon—you just need to know the lay of the land.

In this chapter, you'll learn to what extent American consumers use Amazon as their preferred search engine for products, the impact of advertising (both as a revenue generator for Amazon and a channel for you) throughout the Amazon ecosystem, how to optimally align your company with Amazon as a brand owner, and the path to sustainable success once you've made that alignment.

AMAZON: THE SEARCH ENGINE FOR PRODUCTS

Today, Amazon has become the "everything store" for 310 million customers worldwide, but just as significant, it has eclipsed Google as the place where U.S. consumers start online product searches. According to a Jumpshot report published in September 2018, 54 percent of consumers now start their product searches (the searches consumers make when they know what products they want) on Amazon, not Google.

AMAZON'S ADVERTISING BUSINESS AND YOU

If your brand already advertises on U.S. search engines, can you afford to miss out on more than 50 percent of product searches by not advertising on Amazon?

Amazon may not be considered an ad-supported company (like Google), but according to market research company eMarketer, they are now the third largest generator of digital ad revenue (behind Google and Facebook) in the U.S. In 2018, eMarketer estimates Amazon will bring in $4.61 billion in ad revenue in the U.S., which is more than either Twitter or Snapchat. As Amazon leverages its position as the dominant product search engine in the U.S., over time it will enjoy stronger overall profits.

Consider how Amazon's success as an online ad platform is factored into your current digital marketing strategy. If you're still deciding whether to use Amazon as a key marketing engine for your brand, don't worry—you haven't missed the boat.

Amazon's greatest promotional opportunity for brands big and small is still in its early days, with the use of various categories like Sponsored Products, Sponsored Brands, and, for brands that sell directly to Amazon, Product Display ads. You'll learn more about each of these ad types throughout this book.

As Google has demonstrated, launching paid advertising placements atop a robust organic search engine is nothing short of transformative. Retailers and brands that use search engine text ads and Google Shopping aren't at the mercy of complex, ever-changing ranking algorithms (those results that most closely match the user's search query). Advertising brings predictability and scale to the channel, driving new customer acquisition and revenue growth.

AMAZON IS BRAND CENTRAL

While there are plenty of resellers on the Amazon marketplace who sell products made by other brands, the people who will get the most value from this book will be the brand owners themselves.

In the traditional sense, a brand is a product manufactured by one company under a particular name. More than a century ago, cattle ranchers used a unique branding iron to indicate which cattle were theirs. With the rise of mass-market consumer products, manufacturers and marketers began putting their names on their products to stand out from their competitors. Today, a brand is a collection of promises, both logical and emotional, including qualities and attributes that help consumers inform their purchase.

Whether you are a massive, century-old, well-recognized consumer brand or simply a college student getting started with a line of bamboo fabric surfer T-shirts, you are invisible to almost half of all U.S. consumers if you do not have an Amazon presence.

With your unique brand, you can capitalize on Amazon's continued dominance by either selling *to* Amazon or selling *on* the Amazon marketplace.

Amazon's strong growth pattern, born of vision, innovation, and methodical action, makes it *the* dominant force in online retail, which filters down to benefit your brand. Consumers who previously tolerated sloppy and inconsistent customer service, poor product selection, unexpected back orders, or incomplete product descriptions were impatiently waiting for something better.

The growth of Amazon over the past 24 years should not have taken any smart retailer by surprise. Almost everyone who paid attention to the nexus of the Internet and Amazon could see it coming as plain as day.

KEY BUSINESS DRIVERS FOR AMAZON'S RETAIL GROWTH

From my perspective, there are three key business drivers of Amazon's astonishing rise from an online bookseller to the retail behemoth it is today: Amazon Prime, Fulfillment by Amazon, and the various iterations of AmazonFresh. Let's dive into each of these one by one.

Amazon Prime

In my mind, one of the strongest drivers for Amazon's consumer growth in the U.S. has been its Prime membership. Prime gives members access to free two-day shipping, unlimited video streaming of thousands of popular movies and TV shows, and exclusive shopping deals. Figure 1-1 below, from Morgan Stanley's Amazon Disruption Symposium, shows just how fast Amazon Prime has been growing in the U.S. According to research conducted by Morgan Stanley and reported by *Forbes* in March 2018, U.S. Prime members spend $2,486 a year with Amazon vs. $544 per year for customers without a Prime membership. That's a whopping 4.6 times more.

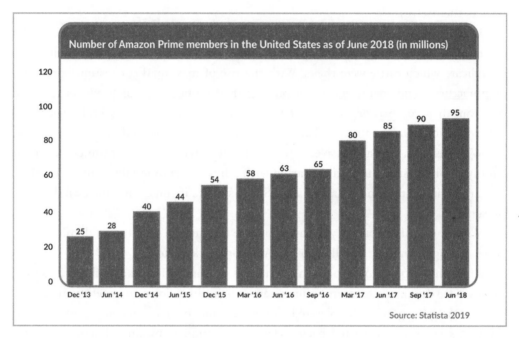

FIGURE 1-1. Amazon Prime U.S. Household Penetration

In the U.S. alone, 95 million households (out of 125 million total) have an active Amazon Prime membership. That's more than two-thirds of all U.S. households. Amazon is where Americans buy.

Fulfillment by Amazon

Fulfillment by Amazon, introduced on September 19, 2006, allows Amazon marketplace sellers to leverage Amazon's order fulfillment and customer service infrastructure—including the ability to store their products in Amazon's distribution centers. Prime customers can take advantage of free two-day shipping when purchasing products in Amazon warehouses, regardless of whether Amazon owns the inventory or a merchant does.

AmazonFresh

Launched in August 2007, AmazonFresh was Amazon's first move toward the grocery business. By this and by its subsequent grocery investments (including its purchase of Whole Foods in 2017), Amazon has showed the business community that being in the grocery business is key for them.

Mastering the grocery business (especially online) boosts Amazon up a significant level from being a seller of packaged goods; after all, not everyone needs to buy books and other "hard" goods, but everyone has to eat.

UNSTACKING AMAZON'S DECK

As I write this, there are 59,721 decks of playing cards for sale on Amazon. Already have a deck of cards? Well, there are about 562 million other items you can buy instead.

In an attempt to understand the scope of Amazon's immense catalog, someone once posted an interesting question on Quora:

> *"How much would it cost to buy one of everything on Amazon?"*

Business researcher Kynan Eng performed some impressive calculations in early 2016 to arrive at a solid estimate: $12.86 billion. That's some number!

But when considering Amazon's scope, one critical fact is hidden from the average consumer: Amazon only makes about half their sales as a first-party retailer. As of Q3, 2018, 53 percent of all paid units on the site were sold by third-party marketplace sellers.

So Amazon takes half the deck and then splits the other half among roughly 2 million sellers competing in their marketplace. If you want to know how to get a piece of either deck, you should understand how the infrastructure for selling on or to Amazon caters primarily to brand owners.

STACKING YOUR DECK

The first step toward stacking the revenue growth deck in your favor is to realize that consumers are loyal to brands, not retailers or sellers. Resellers make one-off sales. Brands can create loyal customers. So you are already one step ahead if your company owns one or more brands.

If you *are* a reseller of products in a specific category, why not begin the journey toward building your own brand?

Early last fall, as I was traveling for one of our ecommerce events, I spent time in the warehouses of two different clients. They were in two distinct parts of New Jersey, and both sold highly commoditized products in their respective categories. Both had been selling on the Amazon marketplace for at least five years. Each had independently switched to branding their products so that they were no longer reselling someone else's products; their packaging now carried their respective logos, brand colors, web addresses, and even their phone numbers.

DON'T HAVE YOUR OWN PRODUCT BRAND?

For retailers of products made by other brands, selling on Amazon isn't as compelling an opportunity. When you sell on Amazon, you're building *their* brand (both the manufacturer's and Amazon's). Amazon and the brand own the relationship with the customer. And, with lower product margins compared to that of the brand owner's, it often isn't profitable to pay Amazon sellers' fees and ad click costs.

Unless you realistically have a shot at becoming a major distribution player in your field (e.g., Walmart, Target, PetSmart, etc.) or have products that due to their size, weight, or need for customization, cannot get marginalized (or outmaneuvered) by Amazon, you want to manufacture products under *your own brand*. Even major distribution players do this over time. Walmart, Target, and PetSmart all have their own house brands.

As a retailer, your strategy takes a bit more planning and investment, but it may be the best in the long run anyway. Take a cue from Amazon. Over the past few years, Amazon has launched their *own* house brands in key categories. Sure, there's the phenomenally successful Amazon Echo, but Amazon also has a number of lesser-known brands, such as AmazonBasics, Happy Belly, Wickedly Prime, and Presto! This is no small move, and it's paying off. For example, AmazonBasics batteries reportedly account for almost one-third of all batteries sold online.

You can have others manufacture your branded products for you, or you can manufacture them yourself. Resist the urge to build your business by only selling someone else's branded merchandise. If someone else owns the brands you're selling, Target, Walmart, or Amazon is—or eventually will be—selling them too.

With a new or emerging brand, you'll have a greater opportunity to get some of those 310 million potential Amazon customers to discover, and then buy, your brand's products.

THE PATH TO GREAT, SUSTAINABLE BRAND SUCCESS

In our hometown of Raleigh, North Carolina, the month of May kicks off the summer concert season. There are so many bands and artists to see. The energy and excitement that comes from hearing your favorite music performed live by the original artist while you're surrounded by friends and neighbors is almost indescribable.

But for every top performer who is hugely successful at what they do (and rich because of it), there are thousands, perhaps hundreds of thousands, of musicians who are struggling, pounding the pavement, and working gigs at small clubs hoping to hit it big.

The same is true in business generally and brand commerce specifically. For every Apple, Staples, Amazon, and Macy's, there are thousands more companies that are just doing OK.

As you consider how best to build your brand on Amazon, think broadly about your game plan for optimal success. Here are a few key strategies to help you focus your efforts on finding even greater success in commerce—whether you're celebrating your fifth year in business or your 50th.

Key 1: You Understand the Mind of the Buyer

You sell products and services where you keenly understand the mind of the buyer. The more you understand the buyer—their needs or desires, what they're willing to pay good money for, why they buy—the easier it will be to make great decisions. If you don't know what they want, then survey them until you do.

At ROI Revolution, we're always asking questions to better serve our clients, and you should do the same. We ask questions like:

- Would you recommend us to your friends and colleagues?
- What about your business keeps you awake at night?
- What was the specific pain you wanted to address just before you hired us?
- What enabled you to eventually trust us?
- What other marketing services do you need or want?

Think of questions to ask customers or potential customers so you can better address their needs and wants.

Key 2: You're Doing Something You Have Intense Enthusiasm For

Have you ever studied the tour calendar for a major band or artist? Lubbock, Texas; Dallas, Texas; Lafayette, Louisiana; St. Louis, Missouri; Noblesville, Indiana; on and on it goes as they crisscross the country in their tour buses and big rigs. Night after night it's the same performance, the same songs, again and again and again.

But when your favorite band comes to play, even if it's the 37th stop of the tour for the artist, for the audience, it's magic. It's as if they came to play just for you and your friends. How do they stay fresh?

In two words: *intense enthusiasm*. A talented artist bemoans the end of the tour. Make sure you're doing or selling something for which you have, or can develop, an intense enthusiasm for. And if you've already created success but lose enthusiasm for your work, the success soon leaves you.

If it's your brand, or if you are in charge of your brand's product expansion strategy, develop and market products you truly believe in and are excited about.

Key 3: You Build and Promote Your Own Brand

Virtually every artist starts out performing covers of other artists' songs in small clubs. However, name one major band or artist who makes performing other bands' popular songs their core repertoire. You can't. Sure, most artists perform some songs by other bands, but it's not their whole act.

The same rule applies to products. It's fine if you start off selling other companies' products, but focus on getting to the point where you're selling your own trademark-protected products (i.e., under your own brand or label).

KAVAJ'S RADICAL "AMAZON ONLY" DECISION

Kavaj, a leather-goods brand, made the radical decision in 2011 to funnel all their online sales through Amazon. Their Facebook and Instagram ads point to Amazon, as does their own website.

Amazon's high conversion rates (the number of sales divided by the total number of visitors: 74 percent for Amazon Prime members, 13 percent for non-Prime members) weren't even the primary reason Kavaj decided to go through Amazon. Their strategy is driven by the fact that every sale they make on Amazon improves the organic rank of their product listings on the site. Given Amazon's massive domination of ecommerce, this high ranking is the focus of Kavaj's ecommerce game plan.

While Kavaj's Amazon-only strategy is extreme, there's no denying that a strong advertising campaign on Amazon can catapult your brand's growth.

AN AMAZON STRATEGY FOR YOUR BRAND

A well-designed Amazon brand strategy does three things:

1. Controls pricing and product distribution (because if you sell products to distributors, you will likely find some or all of them on Amazon, even if you don't deal with Amazon directly)
2. Enhances product listings so your brand is well-represented and consumers are fully informed of what your brand offers
3. Accelerates sales (on and off Amazon) with advertising

I will cover each of these three core strategies in detail throughout this book, starting with getting control of pricing and product distribution in the very next chapter.

Once you understand the first two points, the bulk of this book will be spent on giving you the tools, skills, and mindset to accelerate your brand's revenues and profit with Amazon Advertising.

Chapter 2

How to Control Product and Pricing on Amazon

Honesty and frankness make you vulnerable.

Be honest and frank anyway.

—KENT KEITH, AMERICAN AUTHOR, SPEAKER (1949–)

One of the keys to Amazon's success is the proliferation of consumer-driven product reviews. How many times have you searched for a product on Amazon and studied the reviews before buying (or not)?

Brands can no longer put out slipshod consumer products and expect to prosper like some have in the past. Product reviews are here to stay, and they form the cornerstone of Amazon's draw as a product search engine.

I remember exploring the web for a $200 consumer electronic piece. I saw a promo for it on a client's ecommerce website and got *really* interested in it. But then I read the harsh consumer reviews on my client's site and read more reviews on Amazon. Not good at all. Of course, I didn't buy it, even though the product concept and price point were really attractive. This chapter will look into the push and pull behind getting control over your brand's products and pricing.

WELCOME TO THE AGE OF TRANSPARENCY

In a 2013 *New York Times* article entitled "Social Media as a Megaphone to Pressure the Food Industry," food manufacturers became the "target of complaints that sometimes become magnified in an online environment." The article went on to show how corporations are increasingly capitulating to consumer demands, amplified by the power of social media. It's about time!

For example, one of the most refreshing things I've experienced with Google, ever since my first visit to their Mountain View, California, campus in 2005, is their sincere commitment to transparency. From their auction ad pricing (where no advertiser, no matter how large, is favored over another) to their support of the open-source software movement, Google seems to truly embrace transparency.

Amazon has similarly embraced transparency, at least on the product side. Company founder Jeff Bezos has consistently led a focus on product transparency that ties into their obsession with providing top-notch customer service. Look up any widely popular book that has been out since at least the early 1990s, and you'll see consumer reviews going all the way back to 1996!

Because Amazon puts so much emphasis on product ratings, reviews, and low prices, and because it's very easy for sellers to hide behind an assumed name on the site, it should be no surprise that it's often very difficult for brands to control pricing for their own products, even with a Minimum Advertised Price (MAP) policy in place. MAP establishes the lowest prices at which a brand's authorized sellers are permitted to advertise its products.

You could argue that when Amazon does not clearly identify their sellers (for example, by including their address as well as their company name on the site), they're not living up to their commitment to transparency. And you'd be partly right. But because so many of the 2 million sellers on Amazon are small (close to 50 percent of Amazon sellers have annual revenues of less than $100,000 per year), it's likely they want to protect their privacy. Consider, for instance, a homebased seller who may be selling products on the cheap out of their garage.

And remember, when multiple sellers compete for a sale on Amazon, the result is almost always going to be lower prices.

SATURATION AND PRICING

Take a moment to think about your hometown. Let's say you have a Honda dealer close to your home on one of the busiest roads in town. The next closest Honda dealer is likely in a totally different part of town, if there even is another one. If you want a Honda, you'll probably go to the nearest dealer. As long as you feel you got a fair price, you like the salesperson, and the dealership has a solid reputation, you're going to drive home from there in a new Honda.

However, let's say Honda leadership decides to open 19 other Honda dealers in your town, all along the same road. Or they open four others, and 15 more independent dealers pop up because they purchased new inventory from Honda dealers in other communities. What's going to happen to Honda prices? As a consumer, you'll certainly pay less.

If Honda does not pull back on its move to saturate your town, the incentive to advertise and scale the sale of Honda cars and trucks there will disappear. Over time, it's likely the official dealers will seek a business relationship with a competing car manufacturer that can assure them exclusivity in their area.

On Amazon, if you don't or can't control your brand's product distribution and pricing, you'll be faced with two related problems:

1. Your product will likely be sold for less than you want, as more sellers bring product to Amazon and continually cut the selling price in order to appear in the Amazon buy box. (The "buy box" is the white box that appears on the right side of the Amazon product detail page, where customers can add the item they are viewing for purchase to their shopping cart.)
2. As your product's price drops, your sellers' margins will erode. As sales margins shrink, the incentive for sellers to carry your product line drops precipitously.

GETTING CONTROL OF PRODUCT AND PRICING ON AMAZON

The first of the three major principles of a well-designed Amazon strategy for brands (as initially outlined in Chapter 1) is to control pricing and product distribution. As a brand, there are a number of ways to control pricing on Amazon (and online marketplaces in general).

First, if you are the only source for your product (i.e., there are no other authorized resellers or distributors), you can easily control price. You're essentially the only sales channel. To use another automotive example, it's like Tesla Motors, where there are no franchises or independent dealers (all Tesla stores are factory-owned).

When I ordered a Tesla Model S in early 2016, I had to pay the price set by the Tesla factory. Tesla controlled the price simply by being the sole source. No matter what Tesla store I ordered it from, I had to build my ideal model on their website (which I could do on a computer in their showroom with a salesperson present to answer any questions) and pay a deposit. The process was clean, simple, and completely controlled by Tesla.

You can do this, too, but the tricky part to controlling your brand's pricing online is selling your product to distributors or authorized dealers. Whether your brand is firmly established and popular or you are in the early stages of building it, at some point it will be sold on Amazon. Because it's an open marketplace, Amazon doesn't really care if they get access to your products from you or from a reseller (who may or may not be authorized).

If multiple resellers are competing to sell your brand on Amazon, your product's prices will fall. The best way to counteract this is to engage an experienced trademark attorney with a deep background protecting brand manufacturers in similar situations.

One of the smartest guys I know in the field, attorney Whitney Gibson of the Vorys law firm, who leads their illegal online seller enforcement team, says the best way to protect and grow your brand on online marketplaces involves five core steps:

1. Hand select the sellers you want to approve for selling online via marketplaces.
2. Create a reseller policy for all levels of product distribution (including resellers who buy from your authorized distributors).
3. Create a MAP policy (or fine-tune an existing one). See the section on Transparency earlier in this chapter if you need a refresher on MAP.
4. Differentiate between authorized and unauthorized sellers by including material differences in what each can offer (e.g., authorized sellers' customers have full access to your brand's warranty, customer service, recall assistance, etc.).
5. Monitor sales (via technology and/or by placing test buys), investigate sellers who break policy, and use a graduated enforcement system to step up legal pressure until the seller removes your brand's products.

Gibson says that 50 percent of unauthorized sellers will stop after they receive a cease-and-desist order and 90 percent will stop after they're served a draft complaint.

What's in it for your brand (in addition to clean pricing, solid distribution channels, and strong brand value)? Here are a few examples of results other companies have achieved after implementing Gibson's five-step plan:

- One brand went from selling at 50 percent below MAP on Amazon to selling at MAP compliance in just six months.
- Another increased the proportion of sales made by authorized sellers to 100 percent in three months.
- A third went from 74 percent MAP compliance to 97 percent in two months.

Thus, to win at MAP, uphold brand value, and position your brand for long-term success, your company must effectively execute a comprehensive strategy that fully addresses the five core steps and cuts off any reseller who does not respect your written policies.

Now that I've covered the foundation of our first step in the three-part strategy for brands (getting control of pricing and product distribution), I'm going to show you how to start selling your brand's products on Amazon.

If you already sell your brand on (or to) Amazon and have registered your trademarked products using Amazon's Brand Registry, you can skip the next chapter and simply meet us in Chapter 4.

Chapter 3

Getting Started as a Seller on Amazon

The secret of getting ahead is getting started.

—UNKNOWN

There are many reasons to begin selling your brand's products on Amazon, from the millions of active customers on the Amazon worldwide marketplace to the extremely high conversion rates I cited in Chapter 1. If you have a new brand, you can start selling on Amazon quickly without the need for a stand-alone website.

This chapter will show you how to begin selling your brand on Amazon: which Selling Plan makes the most sense, how to open an Amazon selling account, and how to control your brand's Amazon listings using Brand Registry.

Amazon offers two Selling Plans to get you started. The Individual Selling Plan carries a fee of 99 cents per item sold (plus other fees, which vary by category), and the Professional Selling Plan has a subscription fee of $39.99 per month plus other selling fees.

Those other fees include referral fees (usually taken as a percentage of revenue from products sold, which varies based on the product category and may carry a minimum fee of $1), and for sellers who let Amazon handle product warehousing and shipping for them, Fulfillment by

Amazon (FBA) fees. These include such fees as order picking and packing, shipping cost, packing boxes or envelopes, inner "cushion" packaging, and monthly storage fees.

Not all selling categories are open to Individual Sellers (e.g., fine jewelry, personal computers, and professional services). In addition, the use of feeds, spreadsheets, and other tools to load inventory are only available to Professional Sellers. Figure 3–1 below shows a chart from Amazon's site listing the key differences:

Seller Account Type	Individual	Professional
Monthly Subscription	N/A	$39.99
Per Sale Closing Fee [1]	$0.99	N/A
Access to order reports and order-related feeds	No	Yes
Earn top placement on product detail pages	No	Yes
Sell in 20+ open categories	Yes	Yes
Apply to sell in 10+ additional categories	No	Yes
Customize Shipping Rates	No	Yes
Use of feeds, spreadsheets, and other tools to load inventory	No	Yes

1 in addition to separately stated selling fees

FIGURE 3–1. Differences Between Individual and Professional Sellers

If you plan on selling more than 40 items a month, want to sell your products in the U.S., Canada, and Mexico (rather than simply one of the three), or offer special promotions and a gift wrap option for your products, then go with the Professional Selling Plan.

Once you've decided on a Selling Plan, it's time to open your Amazon selling account.

OPENING A NEW AMAZON SELLING ACCOUNT

To open an Amazon selling account (of either type), simply register for the account of your choice by clicking on the "Sell as a Professional" or "Sell as an Individual" button on the Amazon Services site (https://services.amazon.com/selling/benefits.htm), represented in Figure 3–2 on page 19.

Before you begin the registration process, have the following information handy:

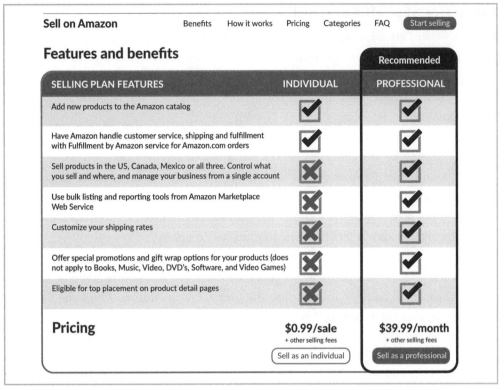

FIGURE 3–2. Register as a Professional or Individual Seller

- Your business name, address, and contact information
- An internationally chargeable credit card (meaning one with a valid billing address in one of the countries Amazon accepts)
- Your bank information, specifically your bank account and bank routing numbers
- A telephone number where you can be reached by Amazon during the registration process
- Your tax identity details
- Information about your products, including answers to the questions below:
  - Do you have Universal Product Codes (UPCs) for all your products?
  - Do you manufacture and brand the products you want to sell on Amazon?
  - How many different products do you plan to list?
- Information about your product categories

After you sign up, you will be asked to complete a two-step login verification process. Once that concludes, you will officially have an Amazon Seller Central account. Let's walk through the basics of what you can expect with that account.

AMAZON SELLER CENTRAL

Amazon Seller Central is where you'll spend much of your time as a seller; it's also where you'll find the tools you need to manage your inventory on the Amazon marketplace. This is where you'll create listings, manage orders, correspond with buyers, get feedback from Amazon about your performance, run reports, set up Sponsored Products campaigns, and more.

Once you're in Seller Central, you should explore the interface, play around in the Help section by searching for topics you'd like to learn more about, and use the Settings menu/User Permissions to add more users from your company if you have other employees who will be working on your Amazon account. By adding users, you can give them access to Seller Central and customize their permissions so they'll have the appropriate system rights for their role at your company.

The first step to adding a user is for you (assuming you're the account administrator) to select the level of user permissions you want them to have and then invite them by adding their email address and sending the user access invitation. Once the new user clicks the link in the invitation email, they're taken to a page that gives them limited access to Seller Central. After the user has access, you can grant them higher levels of permissions by clicking on the "Manage Permissions" button in the User Permissions section of Seller Central.

If you'd like to learn more about Seller Central and selling on Amazon in general, and you prefer a more formal learning process, open an additional tab in your browser and go to the Amazon Seller University: https://sellercentral.amazon.com/learn. Seller University (a curriculum of instructional videos designed to help you master the Amazon marketplace), available to users within Seller Central, will help teach you the details of selling on Amazon, tools and policies for sellers, and the products and services that can help you grow.

To access Seller University, follow the link above or log on to Seller Central, click on "Performance" in the main menu, and then select "Seller University." The page you see should look similar to the one shown in Figure 3–3 on page 21.

These instructional videos and PDF learning documents are very thorough. I highly recommend you and the other members of your team dive in and explore!

AMAZON BRAND REGISTRY

There's one final step that's key to controlling your brand's content on Amazon, and I strongly recommend any brand owner with a registered trademark enable it in the "getting started" section of Seller Central: signing up for the Amazon Brand Registry program. Take a look at Figure 3–4 on page 21 to see where to complete this registration.

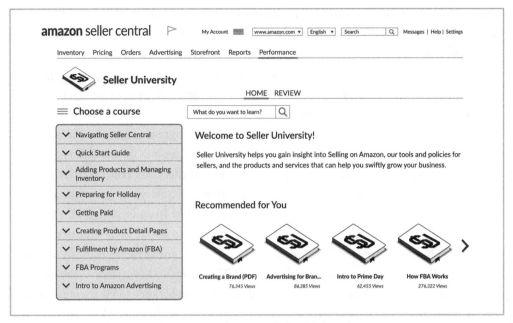

FIGURE 3–3. Amazon Seller University

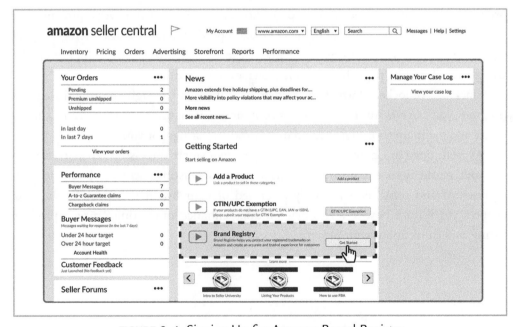

FIGURE 3–4. Signing Up for Amazon Brand Registry

According to Amazon, Brand Registry helps protect your brand's intellectual property and create an accurate and trusted experience for customers on Amazon. With

Amazon Brand Registry, you can have your trademarked brand's Amazon product detail page content locked down so only one marketplace seller (i.e., you or someone who works for you) can alter it.

If you don't register your brand, you can still submit updated or enhanced product content (including images); you'll just have to contact Seller Support for each individual product and have Amazon make the changes for you.

In addition, Amazon says your enrollment in the program gives you access to text and image search tools, predictive automation from your reports of possible intellectual property rights violations, and increased authority (and therefore control) over product listings with your brand name. Finally, Amazon Brand Registry can give you access to Enhanced Brand Content, Amazon Stores, and Sponsored Brands, which all allow you to share your brand's unique story and educate consumers about your products.

James Thomson, former head of Amazon Services, and Joseph Hansen, founder of Buy Box Experts, are co-authors of the book *The Amazon Marketplace Dilemma*. They estimate that "at least 95 percent of all brands have never locked down their content in this manner."

If you don't take control, resellers (authorized, unauthorized, or both) will set up product listings for your products, and they, not you, will determine how your brand promises are communicated to Amazon customers. A reseller will never represent your brand exactly as you would. And because Amazon product page listings often get highly ranked on Google, it's common for many of those listings to show up higher on the Google search results page than a brand's own organic listings.

Once you've locked down your trademarked brands through the Brand Registry program, you can remain responsible for content maintenance or align with a reseller to create and maintain thorough and accurate product listings for your brand.

As mentioned in Chapter 1, the second part of a smart three-step Amazon strategy for your brand is to enhance your Amazon product listings so your brand is well-represented and consumers are fully informed of your brand promises. In the next chapter, you'll learn how to add a new product, enhance an existing Amazon product listing, and think about your pricing.

Chapter 4

Add Products, Then Optimize Your Amazon Catalog Listings

Winners have the ability to step back from the canvas of their lives like an artist gaining perspective. They make their lives a work of art—an individual masterpiece.

—Denis Waitley, PhD, American speaker, writer and consultant (1933–)

As with most things in life, if you want to grow, you're never really done changing. When it comes to your brand, optimizing your product page listings (or your products, for that matter) is an ongoing exercise.

Amazon customers first learn about your product on an Amazon product detail (or catalog) page. The way you present your brand's products on a product page will influence a customer's decision to buy on Amazon.

This chapter will show you how to add one or more of your new products to the Amazon catalog and enhance the listings you already have so your sales increase.

HOW TO ADD A NEW PRODUCT

To create a new listing for one of your products, you can use the "Add a Product" tool on the Seller Central interface. This tool is located in the "Getting Started" section, as shown in Figure 4–1 on page 24.

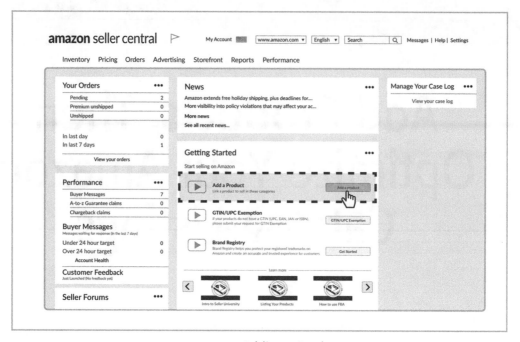

FIGURE 4–1. Adding a Product

You can also find it in the main menu under "Inventory"/"Add a Product," as shown in Figure 4–2 below.

You can use this tool to create a listing for a brand-new product on Amazon, list a small number of your products, or use a simple, step-by-step interface rather than using a spreadsheet in conjunction with Amazon's bulk inventory file template. (This is a

FIGURE 4–2. Adding a Product Under the "Inventory" Link

spreadsheet with multiple data columns for describing your products, available to sellers with Professional Selling Plans.)

For an easy-to-follow, step-by-step guide to using Amazon's "Add a Product" tool, or to learn how to use the bulk inventory upload tool, watch the videos in the "Adding Products and Managing Inventory" section in Seller University: https://sellercentral. amazon.com/learn.

How to Create a New Product Listing

To create a new product listing for a product that is not already in Amazon's product catalog, go into the "List a New Product" tool (Figure 4–3) and choose "Create a New Product Listing" (See Figure 4–4).

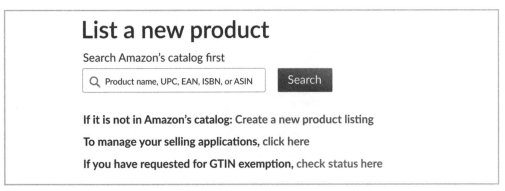

FIGURE 4–3. List a New Product Tool

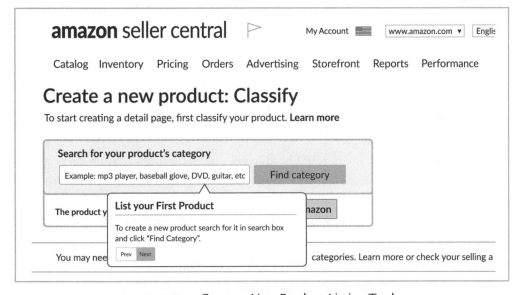

FIGURE 4–4. Create a New Product Listing Tool

You'll then need to find the most appropriate category for your product using the "Search for Your Product's Category" tool, as shown in Figure 4–5. Let's say your company makes jeans—we'd begin with a search for "mens jeans."

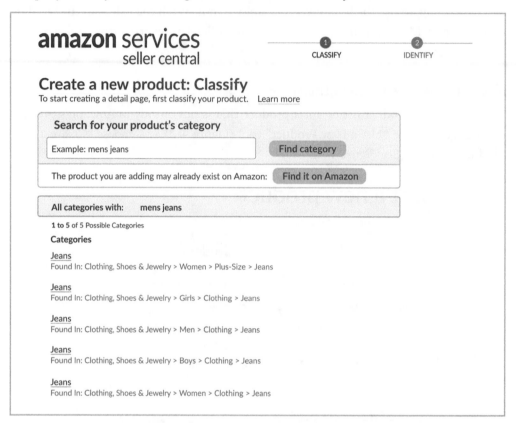

FIGURE 4–5. Create a New Product: Classify Screen

Once you've found the perfect category, click on it to begin entering what Amazon calls "Vital Info" (see Figure 4–6 on page 27). This includes your product's name, product ID, your brand name, and more (the required fields will vary depending on the product category you've selected).

There are three more fields you'll need to fill out, including variation themes (sets of related products, such as size and color variations), offer details (including your standard price and quantity), and images.

To finalize a new product listing, click the "Save and Finish" button at the bottom.

How to List a Product That's Already in Amazon's Catalog

Your brand may already be represented on Amazon if your products are being offered by another seller. For example, you may have a partnership with a known brick-and-

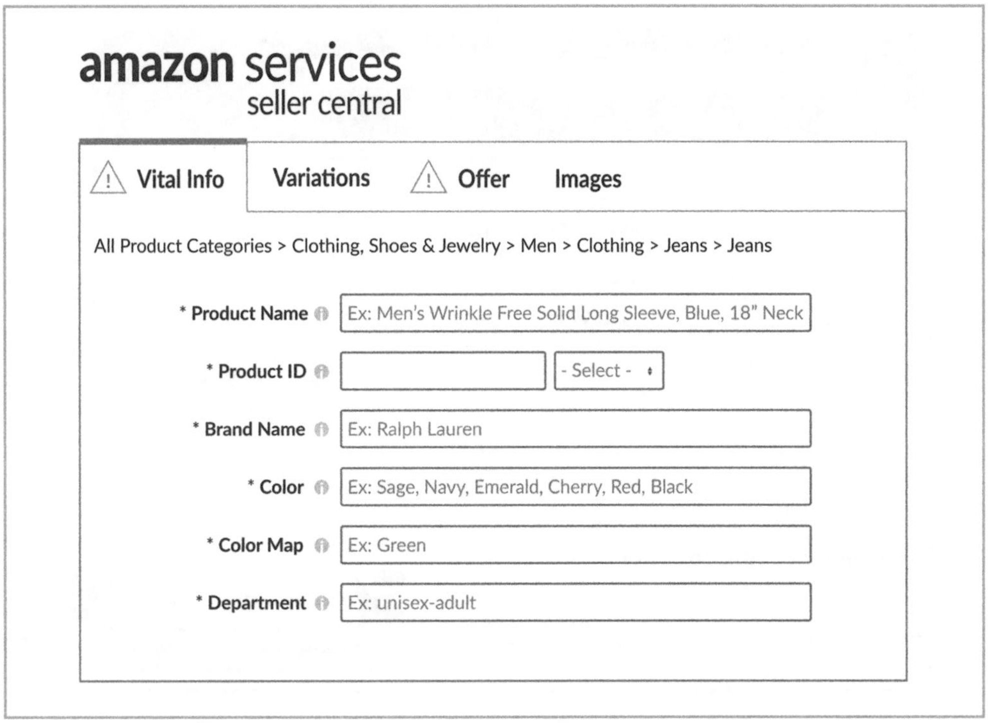

FIGURE 4–6. New Product Listing "Vital Info" Interface

mortar store that happens to fulfill orders on Amazon as well. To see if your product already exists in Amazon's catalog, search for it with the same "Add a Product" tool by entering the product name, UPC, European Article Number (EAN, also known as International Article Number), International Standard Book Number (ISBN), or Amazon Standard Identification Number (ASIN) in the search bar and then click Search.

For example, if you were the brand owner for Duracell, you could type "Duracell AAA battery" in the search bar to see a list of available Duracell brand AAA batteries already listed on Amazon. You could also narrow your results by category on the left-hand menu, as well as search by UPC number. For example, the UPC number for a 16-pack of Duracell AAA batteries is UPC 041333740645. Then click "Sell on Amazon" (as shown in Figure 4–7 on page 28) to list your product under the existing listing. That would take you to an "Offer" page where you can enter your price, condition, and quantity.

The balance of this chapter focuses on how to present your products in the best possible light on Amazon; this advice applies to both new and existing listings. As we're getting started, if you have an existing product listing that you know should be stronger, pay especially close attention to this next section.

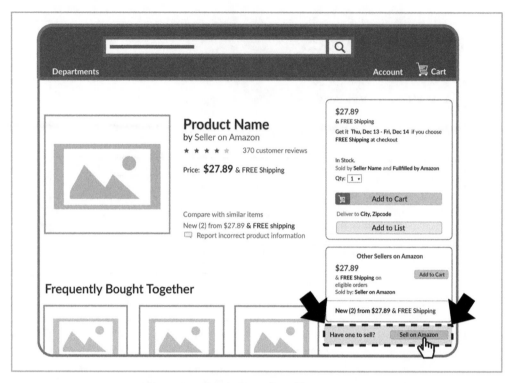

FIGURE 4–7. Sample Offer Page

ENHANCE POOR AMAZON PRODUCT LISTINGS

It's a haphazard world. If you insist on being sloppy, careless, and inattentive to detail, you can usually get away with it. But people who settle for this spend much of their time being disappointed, frustrated, and poorly compensated as a result. That's as true on Amazon as it is in the real world, especially when it comes to product listings.

The range of quality is vast: from product listings with a single, grainy photograph, a few vague bullet points, and zero reviews to highly optimized, lengthy listings with professional photographs, extensive and highly descriptive copy, and thorough technical details.

You want to err on the side of excellence. The more expensive or technical your product is, and providing the market volume exists for it, the more you'll want to increase the time and effort you pour into these listings. Make them your masterpiece.

Provided you've already nailed product quality and have rave reviews from your customers, you've developed inspired branding and product packaging, and you have the supply chain and customer-service infrastructure necessary to support strong sales growth, your success on Amazon starts with a strong catalog product listing.

Sometimes you can fix a not-so-great product listing by doing a little troubleshooting. There are five shortcomings I commonly see with Amazon product listings:

1. Poor product/brand representation, including poor image quality
2. Inaccurate or misleading product claims
3. Unanswered or poorly answered questions
4. Negative reviews
5. Duplicate listings

Let's look at each one in detail.

Poor Product/Brand Representation

Take a moment to look at a listing on Amazon for an Amazon-owned product—for example, an Echo smart speaker with Alexa. Because Amazon owns that brand, they optimize all the selling tools available to them, so looking at their products is a good way to see what best practices for a product listing look like. Note the number and quality of photos, presence of video, and thoroughness of the product description in the top section. Then scroll down; look at the media testimonials, rich sections with very large photographs and additional descriptions, technical details, and the number of customer questions with answers.

While not every product needs the same level of detail that a new piece of technology does, it gives you some insight into how to make a product listing that's on-brand, thorough, and beautiful. It's clear that Amazon has run countless tests to maximize their conversion rates and determine exactly what types of images and information can turn a visitor into a customer.

Inaccurate or Misleading Product Claims

Good business practices on Amazon (or anywhere) mean making accurate and truthful statements. Back in the Wild West days, a traveling snake-oil salesman could say anything he wanted about his product and then move on after pocketing his profits, never to return.

But today, with customer reviews, social media, and the importance of repeat and referral business, every listing requires the utmost honesty and transparency. Scour your existing Amazon listings and make sure they represent your product as well as your brand's main catalog does.

Unanswered or Poorly Answered Questions

Amazon gives buyers and potential buyers an opportunity to ask questions on each product detail page. It's under the "Customer Questions & Answers" section toward the lower part of the page.

In some cases, the questions posed will be answered by existing customers, who already have experience with your product. In other cases, you'll provide the answers. Either way, periodically check for new questions on your pages and proactively answer them.

Negative Reviews

The review score for each of your products should be the consumers' honest reflection of the product's quality, usefulness, packaging, and overall gratification. Obviously, the higher your score, the better. This is why it's key to pay attention to negative reviews and take action where appropriate.

Think about negative reviews in three ways:

1. As an opportunity to get valuable feedback on your products directly from customers so you can learn from them and improve.
2. As an avenue to provide customer service whenever your product, packaging, or documentation has fallen short. You can offer to fix the problem in a way that is visible to other customers.
3. As a chance to spot when a customer may have received a counterfeit product. If you determine this is the case, you can report the situation to Amazon (to cut off the supply of counterfeits going forward) and publicly offer to replace the counterfeit product with a genuine one (which should earn you some goodwill with your customers).

Countering negative reviews in one of these ways will help you maximize the selling potential of each listing.

Duplicate Listings

Amazon's system works by assigning a single ASIN (Amazon Standard Identification Number, a ten-character alphanumeric code used for product identification) per unique product on their marketplace. It creates a poor experience for the customer if the same item is accidentally listed twice under two different ASINs. Someone in your organization may have listed it again, or perhaps it was one of your distributors.

If the additional ASIN is causing a duplicate product listing, you should delete it. This is simple if your company created both listings. Another option is to merge the duplicate product detail pages. If someone outside your team created the duplicate listing and you are the brand owner, you can report the offending duplicate as a violation with Amazon Seller Support. You can merge, delete, or report duplicate violations through the Help menu in Amazon Seller Central.

FIVE ESSENTIAL ELEMENTS OF A HIGH-QUALITY PRODUCT DETAIL PAGE

Now that you know some important caveats about creating individual product listings, let's take a closer look at how you can really make those listings shine. There are five crucial elements of a high-quality product detail page:

1. A descriptive title
2. A beautiful and clear primary product image
3. Clear, concise bullet points
4. An imaginative product description
5. A compelling price

Let's look at each of these in more detail.

A Descriptive Title

Your title should clearly and succinctly describe your product. You should include:

- Your product brand and a short description
- The product line, if applicable
- The material or key ingredient
- Color
- Size
- Quantity (if more than one)

Here's an example of an effective product title (comments in italics):

Tommy Hilfiger *(brand)* Adaptive Collection *(product line)* 100 percent cotton *(material/key ingredient)* Signature Flag Tee (Grey Heather, Small) *(color, size, quantity)*

See how it tells me everything I need to know to make an informed purchase? Remember: Amazon isn't just a place to sell products—it's a place to educate your customers.

A Beautiful and Clear Primary Product Image

A 2018 study by MDG Advertising showed more than 50 percent of consumers value image quality over product descriptions or ratings and reviews. Quality does matter, and a picture actually *is* worth a thousand words. Your main image must have a white background and show the actual product, not an illustration or graphic. Of course you shouldn't stop at just one image—add multiple supporting photos to each listing.

Finally, make sure your product images are at least 1,000 pixels in either height or width (Amazon recommends 2,560 pixels wide) and fill about 85 percent of the frame. This size will enable the zoom feature, which Amazon says can help boost sales.

Clear, Concise Bullet Points

Bullet points highlight key features and important facts that help distinguish your product from the competition. Customers rely on these bullet points to inform their purchase decisions. Focus on the five key features you want your customers to consider. These could include dimensions, age-appropriate range, skill level, ideal conditions for the product, package contents, materials, fit, etc.

Other tips from Amazon for your bullet points include:

- Begin each bullet with a capital letter
- Format each bullet as a sentence fragment (don't use end punctuation)
- Reiterate important information from the title and description where applicable
- Don't include any pricing information (since prices change frequently and bullets are meant to have some longevity in your product detail page listing)

Here are some bullet points describing the Tommy Hilfiger Signature Flag Tee I showed you earlier, taken from a Tommy Hilfiger web page:

- Regular fit
- Ribbed collar
- Magnetic closures at shoulders
- 100 percent cotton
- Imported

You can see how these bullet points fit within Amazon's criteria for a successful product listing.

An Imaginative Product Description

In this section, write a thorough description that captures the customer's imagination, incorporating the look and feel, usage, and benefits of your product in a way that goes above and beyond the information in your bullet points. Use a conversational narrative voice, perhaps the way you'd describe your product to someone over the phone if they had never seen it.

Here's an example of a product description taken from a search result for "cotton canvas pants" on Amazon:

Our Wolverine Fulton pant is constructed from an 8.3 ounce cotton ottoman, which is a uniquely textured fabric that we then concrete wash resulting in a durable, textured, comfortable fabric of choice. This 5-pocket style pant is reinforced with Claw rivets on front and back pocket openings with an additional cell phone pocket on the back right leg.

You can see that the brand manager (or whoever is in charge of this Amazon account) is making the product come alive for the consumer. By talking in detail about your product, you can do the same.

A Compelling Price

With the myriad of choices available on Amazon, there may be no single factor that will determine whether your product is bought by a consumer. Certainly brand reputation, perceived quality, word-of-mouth recommendations, availability, shipping cost/speed, and much more factor into the decision. All things being equal (and of course they rarely are), a compelling price wins.

As an aside, everyday low prices are one of the common threads that tie two of the world's greatest fortunes together: Sam Walton, founder of Walmart (and with his death in 1992, the Walton family as a whole), and Jeff Bezos, founder of Amazon.

As a business strategy, too heavy an emphasis on price is something few firms can pull off. The minimum requirements are economies of scale, tight supply chain management, maniacal cost control, and relentless focus on innovation. And if you're ultimately successful building a brand consumers love and *require*, you're gifted a certain amount of price slack. But your price *does* impact market share, perception of quality, and overall volume, so it's still important to be somewhat competitive.

IMPROVING THE CONTENT ON YOUR PRODUCT DETAIL PAGES

Amazon offers two primary avenues for enhancing content on your product detail pages, depending on your account type. Third-party sellers advertising through Seller Central who have Brand Registry can improve their product listings with Enhanced Brand Content (EBC), whereas first-party vendors through Vendor Central can use A+ Detail Pages to enhance their product detail pages. You will read more about the differences between Seller Central and Vendor Central in Chapter 9.

Both features allow you to enhance your product detail pages in the following ways:

- Tell your brand's story through images, videos, and text
- Highlight brand values and differentiators

- Use images or text to explain how to properly use your product
- Include additional product photos and information for further context
- Proactively address any common questions or concerns shoppers may have regarding your brand or products

Third-party sellers enhance their product pages with Enhanced Brand Content.

Enhanced Brand Content

Enhanced Brand Content (EBC) is only available to third-party sellers who have Professional accounts and have been approved through Amazon's Brand Registry process. EBC is found in the "Product Description" section of the product detail page, where brands typically add large (and small) lifestyle images, product comparison charts, additional text, and other detailed information about their product.

Ultimately, the goal of using EBC is to increase your conversion rate and sales for your brand. You can transform your listing from an ordinary product detail page into one that gives shoppers an introduction to your brand and your products.

With the ever-increasing competition for sales on Amazon, EBC can be the key differentiator between you and your competitors. When it first rolled out, it was a nice option to really make a listing pop, but many companies did not see it as a necessity. Now, as EBC has grown in popularity, it is vital you consider using this feature to stay competitive on Amazon.

You can access this feature by selecting "Enhanced Brand Content" from the Advertising drop-down menu in Seller Central, as shown in Figure 4–8 below. From here, you can select a stock keeping unit (or SKU—a product identification code) that

FIGURE 4–8. Enhanced Brand Content

represents the ASIN you would like to focus on. You can then either select a pre-built template or a custom one. Once you have filled in the template with your images and text, you submit it for approval.

A+ Detail Pages

A+ Detail Pages, which are accessed through Vendor Central, are very similar to EBC but available only to brands selling directly to Amazon. This feature is essentially a tool that allows brands to expand their marketing content on detail pages to include additional text, photos, and charts. A+ Detail Page content appears in the "From the Manufacturer" section of the product detail page. Just like with EBC, A+ Detail Pages serve to catch the attention of shoppers and educate them on the brand message and product features.

Navigate to the "Merchandising" link in Vendor Central to begin creating an A+ Detail Page, as shown in Figure 4–9 below. Select the A+ Detail Pages option from the drop-down menu under Merchandising.

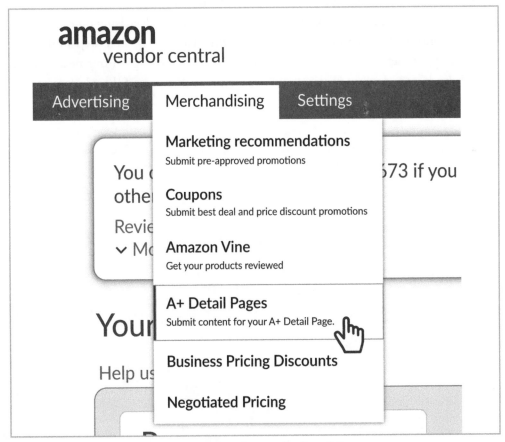

FIGURE 4–9. Starting an A+ Detail Page

You can either create the A+ content on your own through a self-service module, or you can have Amazon handle most of the process on your behalf. It will cost more to have Amazon create the content for you, but the option is there.

If you choose the self-service module, you will need to select the ASIN that you want to create the content for. Then you will select a template and begin adding your images and text to it. You can preview the content before officially submitting it and make any necessary changes based on the preview.

ROCKET FUEL FOR YOUR PRODUCT LISTINGS

By this point, your product pages should be rock solid: great titles, beautiful and clear product images, clear and concise bullet points, imaginative product descriptions, and compelling prices. The next step is to begin to drive traffic (the number of visitors/visits to your Amazon product pages) to your listings.

Of course, it's entirely possible you'll get some free (organic) traffic from Amazon. But organic traffic will only get you so far. The way to really grow revenue, acquire new fans for your brand, and sell more products is by using paid advertising on Amazon.

As I mentioned in Chapter 1, the third and final part of my three-step strategy for your brand is to accelerate your sales with Amazon Advertising. In our next chapter, you'll learn how and why advertising on Amazon is such a powerful tool to grow your brand's product demand and revenue.

Chapter 5

Buy Your Way to the Top:
How Advertising on Amazon Drives Higher Organic Rankings for Your Brand

Trying to do business without advertising is like winking at a pretty girl through a pair of green goggles. You may know what you are doing, but no one else does.

—Cyrus McCormick, American businessman (1809–1884)

Unlike Google (or, for that matter, Bing or Yahoo!), where the paid listings do not affect the organic search results, you *can* (indirectly) buy your way to higher organic placements on Amazon.

As you can see in Figure 5–1 on page 38, advertising on Amazon drives more clicks, more clicks drive more sales, more sales drive more product reviews, and more quality reviews drive a higher organic ranking.

And on Amazon, as in retail in general, this is simply how it should be. Often, there is little true product differentiation for high-selling products over time. Quality and feature parity tend to merge. Consider Kleenex vs. a store-brand tissue, or, on the higher end, consider an Apple iPhone vs. a Samsung Galaxy. In both cases, they are relatively interchangeable in terms of form and function.

The success difference ultimately boils down to marketing (or advertising) and product availability (or distribution).

FIGURE 5–1. The Amazon Advertising Virtuous Cycle

Amazon solves the availability problem for you by offering its massive distribution network of warehouses and fulfillment centers to brands through its Fulfillment by Amazon (FBA) program, which you read about in Chapter 1. Amazon then hands you the keys to accessing its customers and prospects through their advertising programs.

Want to get more attention for your products from Amazon product managers? Turn up the sales volume with advertising. Want to launch new products inexpensively? Launch them first on Amazon, use advertising on Amazon to drive volume to your product listings, and (if successful) extend the launch in more traditional ways (e.g., in-store point-of-purchase displays as well as traditional media campaigns using TV, radio, print, and other digital sources).

IT'S STILL DAY ONE

In Jeff Bezos' first letter to shareholders, written in early 1998, he said, "This is Day 1 for the Internet and, if we execute well, for Amazon.com."

In every shareholder letter since, he has continued to pound home the "it's still Day 1" theme. According to Bezos, "Day 1" means that he always wants Amazon to act like a startup.

For you, when it comes to advertising on Amazon, it's also still Day 1. Here's proof: Do a search for one or more product categories your brand sells on Amazon. Note how most big brands in your space are still missing, and how many lesser-known or smaller brands are advertising there instead. If you're a big brand, why aren't you here? If you're a startup or smaller brand, there are plenty of other smaller brands advertising on Amazon in your category, and you should be here, too!

Recently I searched for products like digital watches, office chairs, gummy vitamins, and bedding sets. Not a single search for any of these product categories contained either a Sponsored Brands or Sponsored Products ad for a well-known U.S. brand, which indicates that the field is wide open for brand owners in these categories to make good use of the available advertising options and, thus, own the "shelf."

In the grand scheme of things, Amazon Advertising, as well as their ad interface, is five to eight years behind Google's. However, I expect Amazon to begin making great strides forward over the next two to three years. For a company like Google or Facebook, advertising is a *very* profitable business, with yearly net profit margins after taxes upwards of 25 percent, so it's a very attractive revenue stream for Amazon to pursue.

In early 2018, on a call with analysts, Amazon's CFO Brian Olsavsky said that advertising was a "key contributor" to the growth Amazon experienced in its North American business in 2017.

Bottom line, for Amazon, the ad business is a win in two ways:

1. Amazon profits on the sale of advertising because of its position as a search engine for products.
2. Because most ads on Amazon direct consumers deeper into the site toward products that consumers can purchase, Amazon is in the perfect position to also capture the sale.

For your brand, advertising on Amazon is a win because:

- You can use advertising to drive product discovery in your category or boost your product listing visibility by encouraging consumers to learn more about your brand's products.

■ According to a 2018 article in *The New York Times*, 70 percent of searches on Amazon are generic (i.e., category) searches. For example, Amazon customers are searching for "ladies sneakers" more than "ladies Nike sneakers" and "men's underwear" instead of "Hanes men's underwear." This means that Amazon Advertising gives you a fair chance to acquire a new client for your brand (big or small).

■ With Amazon's Product Display ads, available to brands that sell products *to* Amazon, you can drive consumers who are at the point of purchasing one of your less expensive products to one with more features, more benefits, and a higher price. You'll read more about this strategy in Chapter 12.

To get your brand in front of Amazon's 310 million-plus active customers, you need a cost-effective strategy that makes sense for your company. The three steps to building an advertising campaign that provides long-term success are: strategy, structure, and optimization.

The next three parts of this book will dive into each of these steps one at a time so you can begin to build effective Amazon advertising campaigns for your brand's products.

Chapter 6

Fleshing Out Your Amazon Business Objectives and Measurements

If you are not making the progress that you would like to make
and are capable of making, it is simply because your
goals are not clearly defined.

—PAUL J. MEYER, AMERICAN AUTHOR AND SPEAKER (1928–2009)

The first pillar in your Amazon ad campaign planning involves fleshing out your specific Amazon business objectives—essentially, the big-picture objectives that align with your overall business goals. If you work for a very large company, this may involve buy-in from senior leadership and take more time than if you work for a small company or for yourself.

In my experience, the key to making great progress in business is having clear, worthwhile, focused, and inspiring objectives.

While my son Brandon was away at college, there were several books we read at the same time and then talked about over the phone at the end of the week. One of the books we read during his senior year was Walter Isaacson's biography of Apple cofounder Steve Jobs.

One of the most interesting stories in the book, which is useful for establishing your quarterly objectives, was how Jobs literally rescued the company from irrelevance upon his return to Apple in 1997. At that time,

Apple was producing a diverse catalog of computers (including a dozen versions of the Apple Mac) and accessories. The story goes that after a few weeks of reviewing products, he made a two-by-two grid and had his team put their best products in each of the four boxes and cancel the rest.

The stunned Apple team did just that, and Jobs' keen eye for focus saved the company. Today, nearly every product Apple makes can be neatly laid out on a single showroom-size display table.

Near the end of Jobs' life, he met with Larry Page (cofounder of Google) and gave Page nearly the same advice for Google: focus, focus, focus. Shortly after, Page began telegraphing a message of "more wood behind fewer arrows" as he sunset a multitude of scattered initiatives at Google, creating a powerful focus behind a vital few.

You'll want to apply this same approach when setting your Amazon advertising objectives.

Success on Amazon means different things to different companies. In this chapter, we will explore three of the most common objectives brands pursue, how to determine quarterly objectives, discuss key performance indicators (KPIs) you may wish to track, and share the way we help our clients think about their overall Amazon advertising cost of sale metric.

Here are three of the most common objectives you may wish to choose from:

1. *Promote your brand.* Worldwide spending on advertising in 2017 is estimated at $550 billion. The U.S. had ad spending of $205 billion in 2017, and Procter & Gamble alone spent $10 billion worldwide on advertising. Clearly, promoting your brand to increase revenue and gain new customers is a big goal of many firms, especially those selling consumer products.

2. *Get rapid growth.* For virtually every product category, there exists a window of time where there is rapid growth. During times of double- to triple-digit annual category growth, some leaders emphasize a "go big" strategy, with the goal of grabbing as much market share as possible. If that's your company's current stage and you have the capacity to fulfill demand, this can be a rare opportunity to establish market dominance.

3. *Get sales at a target return.* In many scenarios for brands, growth and increased brand awareness are desirable, but a target return rate is paramount to gauging ad success. Whether your brand has strict product margins that cannot be encroached on by spending money on ads or the Amazon channel must "prove itself" with exceptional profitability before receiving a higher ad budget, establishing these goals early is incredibly important as reaching your target return range is not instantaneous.

You can come up with other goals or employ a combination of these; however, it's important to establish clear objectives at the start so everyone in your company who is involved with your Amazon strategy is on the same page.

Now that we've talked about the most common overall objectives brands pursue, let's bring it closer to home and discuss selecting your objectives for the upcoming quarter.

DETERMINE YOUR OBJECTIVES FOR THE QUARTER

To begin, you'll want to define two to three objectives (remember, more wood behind fewer arrows) for the quarter that:

- Align with your defined Amazon business goals
- Are screened against your completed competitor analysis
- Are measured against your KPIs

Next, select the products to be promoted through advertising that align with those objectives. For example:

- Products with a high profit margin
- Products you want to clear out of your inventory (similar to how companies have used eBay to clear unwanted inventory)
- Products you want to use to grow your overall rank in Amazon's organic search results
- Seasonal merchandise going into peak season
- Products you want to defend against competitors by placing ads on your most popular Amazon catalog listing pages
- Products that are a "natural" upsell option from high-volume products with a lower price and smaller feature set

Also consider the product's rating on Amazon when deciding which products to advertise. You should aim to advertise products that have at least a 3.5-star rating. Any products with ratings below that are less likely to convert to sales. Think about it: Would you be more likely to buy a product with a two-star rating or a four-star rating?

By breaking out your smaller objectives into specific quarters, you'll accomplish your broader objectives over time.

EXAMPLE OF APPLYING QUARTERLY OBJECTIVES

Here's the story of a company I work with that made leveraging product display ads for upsells and defending against competitors' traffic two of their quarterly objectives.

Polk Audio manufactures audio products; they're best known for their speakers. The company was looking for new ideas and advertising strategies to implement in their very competitive product space on Amazon.

Polk found it difficult to manage their account consistently and implement best practices. They were unsure how their investment in Amazon advertising was driving business, so they didn't know where to invest more and where to trim back. They wanted assurance that their ad dollars were being used as effectively as possible to drive great results and maintain a strong brand presence against competitors who were trying to steal their traffic by advertising against Polk Audio keywords and product pages.

Our Amazon ad team worked closely with Polk to determine which products to push and which to pull back in specific categories. Additionally, more hands-on work on the account allowed for more control over bids, and we decided to increase spending on their bestselling products to win clicks in category searches and defend their traffic in brand searches (by placing ads strategically to lock out Polk's competitors).

Because Polk sells similar products in multiple price and feature tiers, our team set up Product Display ads to help upsell shoppers, using either higher-priced main products or lower-priced Polk items as add-ons to their main product. For example, Polk offers multiple upgraded models of their popular sound bars that are as much as $50 more for a similar product (for an upsell option), and they also offer smaller speakers that could complement the shopper's main purchase.

After months of scaling revenue and profit by increasing investment in their account, during Q4 2017, overall brand keyword-driven orders increased seven times over Q4 2016 at the same cost of sale (which was their goal for brand searches).

Once you've identified your most important two or three objectives and have built your ad structure within the interface (we'll discuss that in detail later in the book), you'll need to be able to measure your progress. That's where performance metrics come in.

ESTABLISH PERFORMANCE METRICS

You can't tell how well you're doing unless you can measure your performance, and you can't do *that* until you decide what exactly you're trying to measure. I'll start with a broad overview of performance indicators, then discuss a key metric unique to Amazon, and finally propose a new metric I believe is the best way to look at advertising expenditures vs. total return.

Key Performance Indicators

Key performance indicators (KPIs) are measurable, quantifiable numbers typically used by marketers and business executives to track their company's performance against their goals. Examples of KPIs include revenue, conversion rate, total ad costs, and total payroll. As part of your Amazon ad strategy, decide which KPIs are most important to track. Then track and report on them to those people who are most responsible for driving their success. In Chapter 19, we'll take a deep dive into the most common KPIs we track for our clients.

Advertising Cost of Sales

The advertising cost of sales (ACoS) is a key Amazon metric many sellers hold near and dear. It's the ratio of direct advertising spending to the sales directly triggered by that spending, and it is calculated like this:

$$\textbf{ACoS = Ad Spend} \div \textbf{Sales}$$

For example, if you spent $10,000 on Amazon ads last month and generated $50,000 in sales attributed to those clicks, your ACoS is 0.20, or 20 percent.

Take extra care when considering your target ACoS. Because digital marketing is so easily tracked, executives often simply pick a target ACoS and measure their Amazon campaign against this single metric. When Amazon marketing is optimized to this goal, the executive is happy—but an acceptable ACoS does not necessarily equal profit. A 10 percent ACoS may look good on paper, but companies grow based on actual profits. Every product you sell generates a specific gross margin (i.e., revenue – cost of goods), but if there is not sufficient gross margin generated from your total sales to pay your overhead costs (also known as sales, general, and administrative costs), you won't make money. Assuming adequate margins, what executive wouldn't rather have 500 sales at a 20-percent ACoS vs. 75 sales at a 10-percent ACoS?

As a general rule, there's an inverse relationship between the potential traffic volume and the ideal target ACoS. The more targeted traffic available, the more competitors move in to squeeze (or increase) the expected ACoS.

Great advertising structure, along with intelligent and ongoing optimizations, will certainly help boost your ACoS. The best strategy, however, involves unlocking *all* the potential in the marketplace. You won't know the volume potential without testing how much profit returns from different levels of advertising spend.

Additional ad spend at a higher ACoS may bring you additional customers, but you could come away with a slightly lower initial profit overall. There are three reasons this may be better for your brand in the long run:

1. *Remember customer lifetime value (CLV).* Your marketing budget needs to account for the lifetime value of a customer. Of course, you need a sizable amount of working capital to pull this off, but paying to win over new customers to your

brand is a fantastic investment when you know that a healthy percentage of those customers will become repeat buyers, paying back that investment many times over.

2. *Happy customers tend to multiply.* Any good brand benefits from some level of viral marketing. Happy customers tell others. Since you paid for the initial customer, any additional customers brought to you through their word-of-mouth advertising are a gift. The more customers your brand wins, the more of these "gifts" you'll receive.

3. *You want to dominate your market.* Every customer you win is a customer lost by a competitor. This drives up your competitor's marketing costs and edges them out of the market. Every market seems to be dominated by two or three big dogs, and you want to be one of them. If it helps motivate you, think of the other side: Every customer you lose because of an overly conservative target ACoS is a customer won by a competitor.

Exploring TACoS

I'd like to propose a new unique performance metric to consider while scaling your brand on Amazon. That's the total advertising cost of sales (TACoS). TACoS is calculated by dividing all Amazon ad costs by your total sales revenue on Amazon, regardless of its source (i.e., paid or organic). This metric contextualizes your ad spend at a much higher level and can bring clarity on where the hard limits for your ad spend are, even in the most aggressive of growth plays. On the other hand, if your TACoS calculation comes out to an exceptionally low percentage (for example, below 5 percent), you can most likely afford to increase your ad investment.

This metric may sound familiar. Many brand managers use it to budget and evaluate ad spending, but they refer to it by another name (we've heard it called "trade spend," for example). Regardless of what you call it, this metric can be valuable when evaluating your overall investment in Amazon ads.

PERFORMANCE AGAINST KEYWORD TYPES

In our agency, we like to look account wide at keyword themes against three distinct buckets: brand, category (upper-funnel marketing to build new demand for your branded products—sometimes referred to as "nonbranded" or "brand awareness"), and competitor terms (bidding on your competitors' brand terms).

There are two main reasons we look at these buckets this way:

1. An overall target performance metric, with a heavy volume in brand keyword-driven ads, can hide unprofitable spend in the other two buckets.

WHERE SHOULD YOU FOCUS YOUR MARKETING INVESTMENT?

About 13 years ago, I went to see famed direct-response marketing guru Dan Kennedy speak in Cleveland, Ohio. During the time when audience members could ask him questions, I walked up to the microphone in front of a packed-house ballroom.

I had been dabbling in five or six different marketing channels of various cost, reach, and ROI assumptions. I already had my favorite, but I wanted Kennedy to give me some final confirmation before I focused my efforts on the best one or two.

"Where should I focus my marketing investment?" I asked. The abrupt response he shared with me that day has formed the core of how we approach marketing for our own company.

This was his answer: "Do it all!"

Sure, he told me, you want to be driving as much volume as possible from your best-performing channel. But assuming you have the capital to invest, you should be investing in *every single profitable channel*.

Businesses stagnate when the definition of "profitable" is restricted to "returns profit at my top ROI target." Profitable means "returns profit." There is incredible business value in customers. Customers become repeat customers, referral champions, and ambassadors of your brand. New customers increase your market share while reducing the market share of your competitors. *Do it all*.

2. If you fixate on a specific overall performance metric average, assuming strong margins, then over time, as your category becomes more competitive, you'll spend less and less on the upper-funnel marketing that's essential to growth (i.e., you'll reduce spend in the category and competitor search buckets). This will seem good on paper, as your overall performance stays constant, but unfortunately, you're not growing your business.

By breaking out these three categories, you'll get clarity on the profitability of or investment in each. This also provides insight into how aggressive each strategy is and gives you a benchmark for investment between the three strategies.

Brand Keyword Terms

Generally, you can expect brand keyword traffic to perform at a lower ACoS (i.e., more profitably) than traffic that is focused on category or competitor search.

Brand keywords are likely to have a higher conversion rate, given the higher purchase intent when someone is searching specifically for your brand. This bucket also includes ad placements that involve cross-branding or upselling. The goal of going after your brand's traffic is brand defense; it aims to drive sales at your target performance rate.

One example of brand keyword traffic would be Calvin Klein bidding on the search term "Calvin Klein dress" (either in Amazon Sponsored Products, Sponsored Brands, or both), which would help block competitors from showing up on searches for "Calvin Klein." They could also use Product Display ads to cross-brand or upsell on their own product detail pages. For example, they might advertise a pair of heels on their product detail page for a cocktail dress. This cross-branding strategy also limits the chance of a competitor stealing a sale by advertising on the product detail page.

Category Keyword Terms

Category traffic refers to search queries and keywords that are not specific to one particular brand but are instead general category-level searches and keywords (for example, "cocktail dress" rather than "Calvin Klein cocktail dress"). The category keyword bucket aims to go after nonbrand-loyal customers by targeting category-level keyword traffic. This strategy can be used in Amazon Sponsored Products and Sponsored Brands ads. The goal is to introduce shoppers to your brand and grow market share. Recall in Chapter 5 the *New York Times* article stating that about 70 percent of the word searches on Amazon are for generic terms. This should be a big part of your brand's customer acquisition strategy on Amazon.

To continue with the Calvin Klein example, they may want to target category keywords such as "crewneck dress." It is important for brands to target category traffic so they can grow brand awareness and increase market share. If a shopper is searching for a generic product, why not go after a chance to gain a new loyal customer?

Competitor Keyword Terms

The third bucket focuses on increasing market share by going after your competitor's traffic. This strategy tends to have a higher cost per sale than brand or category keywords since you are trying to convince someone that they should purchase your product instead of your competitor's.

If Calvin Klein were interested in targeting its competitors on Amazon, the company might want to target keywords such as "Ann Taylor dress" as well as targeting specific product detail pages of Ann Taylor dresses that are comparable to their own products. Competitor keyword targeting can be achieved through Amazon Sponsored Products and Sponsored Brands ads, while product targeting can be accomplished with Product Display ads. We'll talk more about each of the three Amazon ad types starting in Chapter 10.

In our next chapter, we'll scope out what your competitors are doing as a way to inform your overall Amazon strategy.

Chapter 7

Competitive Analysis Time

> *Do your work with your whole heart, and you will succeed—*
> *there's so little competition.*
>
> —ELBERT HUBBARD, AMERICAN WRITER (1856–1915)

It's time to figure out what your competitors are up to! In this chapter, I'll build my case for being customer-centric, outline the need for a competitive analysis, discuss third-party tools you can use, and outline six specific questions to ask yourself to help determine your competitive position on Amazon.

When Amazon launched in 1995, it was with the mission to be "Earth's most customer-centric company." While it's prudent to study what your competitors are up to, combining competitive analysis with a passion for serving the customer is my definite business bias.

While the lion's share of competitive analysis is outward-facing, I tend to be more inner-focused, thinking about how I can innovate on behalf of my customers so I can delight and wow them. It's another way of expressing love for your customers and their needs, rather than just a means to *your* goals.

What data, if any, backs up the value of great customer service? A 2012 study conducted by Watermark Consulting using the data in Forrester's

KING BEZOS

Love him or hate him, Amazon's Jeff Bezos reigned supreme in customer service for nine years. According to an online retailer study by customer experience analytics firm Foresee, Bezos led the company to the highest customer satisfaction score from 2004 through 2013, and in 2017, Amazon topped the Internet retail sector for highest American Customer Satisfaction Index (ACSI) score.

Customer Experience Index showed that a portfolio of customer-experience leaders had a return of 22.5 percent. During that same period, the S&P 500 declined 1.3 percent, and a portfolio of customer-experience laggards declined 46.3 percent.

Brand, retail, and ecommerce executives come to my company and other companies like it to get better results from their digital marketing with less worry and pain. But sometimes, their thorniest business problems can be solved by focusing on the customer, rather than focusing on their competitors.

Great customer service leads to increased credibility, results in word-of-mouth advertising, and boosts revenue, especially for retail and ecommerce, where decent customer service is the minimal expectation.

At the end of the day, your ability to attract new customers, retain existing ones, and allow customers to multiply themselves through referrals, reviews, and social media comments is all you have.

Customer service is at the heart of what you do as a brand. By centering your thinking on customer service, you are better positioned to investigate and analyze what your competitors are doing in the Amazon space. Let's start by getting a reality check on the marketplace for the categories you compete in.

PERFORM A COMPETITIVE ANALYSIS

If you've spent any time in marketing or read some books on marketing, you've undoubtedly heard of a SWOT (strengths, weaknesses, opportunities, and threats) analysis.

A SWOT analysis is a useful technique in business for teasing out your company's most prominent profit and growth opportunities as well as its unique strengths. While it may be common sense to work on strengthening your weaknesses, the real money in business is leveraged by *strengthening your strengths*.

Strengthening Your Strengths

A number of years ago, I read an article in an airline magazine by Hayagreeva Rao, originally published in the *Harvard Business Review*, that illustrates this point perfectly. It was so provocative and useful that I've reread it at least a dozen times, maybe more.

The article examines the progressive manner in which 17th-century pirates managed the assignment of job duties. This dark time in human history provides somewhat surprising insights on business. Rao describes how all business tasks can be roughly categorized into one of two buckets: star tasks and guardian tasks.

Star tasks represent any strategic work that provides leverage to grow and expand. In the case of pirates, this would be tasks such as identifying new targets and negotiating alliances, handled by the ship's captain.

Guardian tasks represent operational responsibilities that keep an organization operating smoothly. For pirates, this would involve distributing rations, inflicting punishment to crew members, allocating looted goods, and mediating conflict, all managed by the quartermaster general.

Here is the meat of the story: star tasks and guardian tasks require completely different human skill sets. While each is critical to a healthy organization, it's rare to find someone who excels at both. Instead, people tend to gravitate to one or the other. If a job role requires a bit of each, as is common, one group of tasks is almost always neglected in favor of those deemed easier or more interesting.

In my company, I focus on the star tasks (sales, marketing, and vision), and my COO focuses on the guardian tasks (operating the business). This is the same way that Steve Jobs focused primarily on product innovation and marketing at Apple while his COO (now Apple's CEO), Tim Cook, handled everything that related to operations, manufacturing, and distribution.

The big takeaway is that you can make more money faster and more easily by strengthening your strengths (including capitalizing on the strengths of your products) than by spending a lifetime trying to perfect your weaknesses.

Here are six Amazon-specific questions we like to ask our clients when helping them form their unique strategy:

1. *How competitive is your category?* Gauging the competitiveness of the product categories in which your brand will sell is paramount to establishing a sound Amazon strategy. Most product categories will continue to experience rising cost per click (CPC, the price you pay for each ad your prospects and clients click on) as the marketplace grows and more established brands move into the space, but some have already gone through sizable increases. A client of ours in the home decor category has experienced this competition firsthand. At the start of our management relationship, the average

TAKE YOUR COMPETITIVE ANALYSIS TO THE NEXT LEVEL

There are a lot of powerful (and not so powerful) third-party tools for Amazon sellers that can help strengthen everything from your brand equity to your keyword analysis and tracking to your competitive research. Many of these tools have some degree of overlap and various strengths and weaknesses. My recommendations are below.

Tracking and Moderating Reviews

Amazon doesn't notify sellers when they get a negative review, so you need a third-party tool for tracking any negative reviews. According to a 2015 survey by global marketing firm Mintel, nearly 70 percent of consumers consult online reviews before they make a purchase, so a negative review on your listing can have a large impact on conversion rates.

In some highly competitive product categories on Amazon, some sellers have been known to leave unverified negative reviews on their competitors' listings. You will want to be vigilant about these types of reviews and submit a ticket to Amazon disputing the review as soon as you spot it. For verified negative reviews, your "customer is always right" mentality must come to the fore. Use the comment feature to address negative reviews head-on, kindly acknowledging the issue that the consumer has raised and providing a solution or reiterating your brand's commitment to a great user experience. For assistance in tracking reviews and receiving notifications of negative reviews, I'd recommend the FeedbackFive tool (https://www.feedbackfive.com).

Increasing Reviews

If you have new listings without any reviews, it can be hard to gain momentum. Many Amazon customers need verification that somebody else has bought a product and seen that it works properly before they will take a chance on it themselves. This increases in lockstep with the price point. Coupled with one estimation that only 5 percent to 10 percent of Amazon shoppers leave product reviews, that means getting your first review can be difficult. So when you're launching a product, getting those initial reviews is paramount.

For help increasing and soliciting reviews from recent purchasers, I recommend the Feedback Genius tool (https://www.sellerlabs.com/feedback-genius).

TAKE YOUR COMPETITIVE ANALYSIS TO THE NEXT LEVEL, continued

Tracking Bestseller and Keyword Ranking

Tracking your organic rankings and how your keywords are ranking relative to your competition is very important for gauging the effectiveness of your advertising campaigns. There are many components that go into determining Best Sellers Rank (BSR), including review count and quality, recent sales velocity, organic sales, and listing conversion rate. With that said, one of the more direct ways to drive your BSR up is increased ad presence. Measuring the effect of this can be tough, but there are tools to give you a picture of what may or may not be working. For better tracking your BSR, I would recommend the AMZFirst tool (https://www.amzfirst.com).

Analyzing Competitor Listings and Sales: Staying up-to-date with what the competition is doing is incredibly important in a fast-paced and competitive marketplace such as Amazon. Discovering which keywords your competition is consistently ranking for, as well as tracking any large changes to their listings, can keep you a step ahead of your competitors as their internal strategies evolve. For help with tracking the changes your competition makes to their listings, I recommend Helium 10 (https://www.helium10.com).

CPC for one of their keyword-driven ads was 78 cents. A year later, that CPC now sits just shy of $1. Since the costs advertisers pay in a CPC model on Amazon are based on competitive bidding for placement, as more advertisers enter the space, the cost per click inevitably goes up.

2. *What is your fulfillment strategy vs. your competitors'?* For example, are you or your competitors using Fulfillment by Amazon (FBA), which is where you send your products to the Amazon fulfillment centers closest to your customers and Amazon stores, picks, packs, ships, and provides customer service? With FBA, your products become eligible for Amazon Prime and free shipping (on qualifying orders) with the option for gift wrapping and an up-to-the minute countdown on one-day shipping.

3. *How are your product reviews vs. your competitors' (both in quantity and quality)?* Product reviews are king on Amazon. No amount of advertising can sustainably increase conversions for a product with an exceptionally poor rating. It is important to track

both the quality and quantity of your product's ratings relative to the competition. Moderating your product's review section by screening for unverified reviews and personally commenting on any negative reviews is a great way to mitigate any damage to product or brand perception as a result of mixed or negative reviews.

4. *What is your listing quality vs. your competitors'?* Listing quality is a large factor for customers when deciding to purchase a product on Amazon. *Does this product come from a reputable source? What kind of brand is selling me this product?* These are the questions new customers may have when deciding to purchase your product, and a well-built and maintained listing can answer them. Perhaps the overall quality of listings in a product category is particularly low when compared to other, more established categories: blurry pictures, poor keyword indexing (i.e., a small number of relevant keywords in product titles or descriptions), or a significant lack of brand content and graphics. This could be an opportunity for your product and its new or improved listing to shine in comparison.

5. *What is your pricing compared to your competitors'?* On Amazon, customers have exceptionally high expectations—free shipping, unmatched customer service, and the lowest possible prices. According to a 2016 study from retail search consulting firm CPC Strategy, 23.1 percent of U.S. internet users cited price as the deciding factor when making a purchase on Amazon, making it the largest factor.

6. *How are your products bundled compared to your competition?* You may choose to bundle certain products in your catalog, both for customer convenience and an improved margin. This is a highly successful tactic on Amazon and falls in line perfectly with the marketplace's "one-stop shop" theme. A client of ours in the personal beauty and care category created a bundle that mixed a small selection of very high-margin fragrance products with a lower-margin electronic diffuser. They priced this product at a significant premium compared to their competition's diffuser-only offering, but it was enormously successful due to its "starter pack" nature. The listing now consistently ranks higher than their competitor's singular offerings. Ask yourself these questions when considering a bundle option for your products: *Is this price competitive with my competition's bundle offerings? Has this mix of products proved successful elsewhere? Does this improve my margin?*

Now that you have clarity on your product's strengths as well as how your brand's products stack up against your competitors', it's almost time to start building an effective ad structure within the Amazon Advertising interface. But first it's important to learn how to mine and discover keywords around the products you've prioritized for the quarter.

Chapter 8

Keywords and Keyword Research

Creativity requires input, and that's what research is.
You're gathering material with which to build.

—Gene Luen Yang, American cartoonist (1973–)

At its core, Amazon is a shopping search engine. Customers search for products by using a specific combination of terms that they believe will deliver them a selection of goods to choose from. Amazon's search engine algorithm then serves up what it thinks is the most relevant search results for the shopper based on the term or phrase they used. As you can see in Figure 8–1 on page 58, within the search results page there are three types of results: Sponsored Brands, Sponsored Products, and organic listings.

Pay-per-click (PPC) advertisers take advantage of the flow of customer search term traffic by selecting and bidding on keywords through which to advertise their products. Every time a shopper types a term into the search box, an auction is held between advertisers who have previously bid on related keywords. The sponsored ads are then placed in various spots on the search results pages with higher bids winning the more prominent ad slots and less competitive bids populating the remaining slots further down the page (and subsequent pages). This entire process occurs in

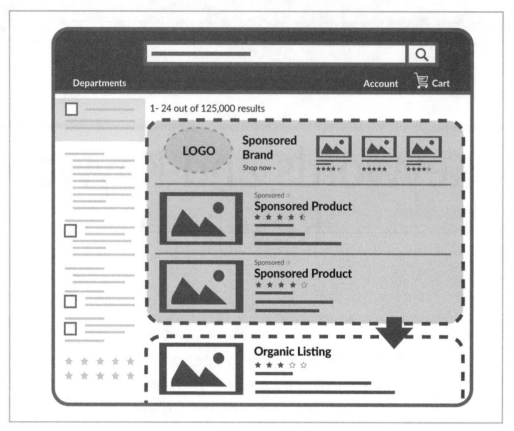

FIGURE 8–1. Three Product Results

milliseconds as the shopper's search results load, sponsored ads first, with the organic results typically falling well below the fold (the portion of a web page that is only visible after scrolling down).

The keywords you choose to bid and advertise on are the backbone of your Amazon advertising campaign (I'll cover bidding extensively starting in Chapter 14). Keywords are the primary window through which Amazon shoppers discover and purchase your products. This is why, in many ways, keyword research is a very basic form of market research. By continuously researching and discovering new ways that customers are searching for your products and other products in your category, you are staying up-to-date on what customers are thinking when searching, and even where their preferences might be heading.

In this chapter, I'll help you understand the foundation for the key driver of those search results (keywords) and how to use them effectively in your Amazon campaigns. To begin, let's talk about the types of keywords you will use to bolster your brand.

KEYWORD MATCH TYPES

In an attempt to capture every iteration, variation, and evolution of a customer search term, the keywords you use are broken down into three match types: exact, phrase, and broad.

Exact Match

Exact match is the most specific and targeted match type on Amazon. There is a common misconception that exact match keywords target only the exact keyword or phrase you have selected, but our Amazon Advertising team has concluded that it also targets plural variations of the word or phrase. For example, an exact match keyword for "mattress pad" will also catch customer search queries for "mattress *pads*." In fact, *all keyword match types* will catch plural variations. On the other hand, exact match keyword will not catch slight misspellings of terms. For instance "vacuum" will not catch "vaccuum." You will need to build out separate keywords to catch common misspellings like this. This is especially important if you have a commonly misspelled brand name.

Aside from these small variations, exact match only captures traffic that matches the keyword in the same word order. For example, an exact match keyword for "mattress pads" will *not* capture "pads mattress." They will also not capture any additional words within a customer search term, so a "mattress pads" exact match will not capture a term such as "hypoallergenic mattress pads." In order to capture important terms like these, you will need to use phrase match keywords.

Phrase Match

Phrase match keywords slightly widen your net to capture more search term traffic. A phrase match keyword will capture traffic with any variation of a keyword or keyword phrase as long as the words that trigger the search term are in the same order as the keyword you've added. For example, a phrase match keyword for "mattress pad" will capture the search term "waterproof mattress pad" because it contains the words "mattress pad" in that order. Conversely, the phrase match keyword "mattress pad" will not capture "waterproof pad for mattresses" because the search term does not contain "mattress pad" in that specific order. Phrase match keywords are great for discovering new variations for high-volume keywords that customers might be using to search for your products.

Broad Match

Broad match keywords are the widest net you can cast within your Amazon ad campaigns. For a customer search term to trigger a broad match keyword, the search term must contain the individual words that are in the keyword, but in no particular order. For example, the broad match keyword "mattress pad" will capture a search such as "pad for twin mattress" because it contains the terms "mattress" and "pad," even though they're in a different order. Broad match keywords can act as a further discovery tool for new phrases customers may be searching.

Now that we have covered the various keyword match types that will capture your customer search term traffic, let's cover how to properly group and prioritize those keywords by further categorizing them by *traffic theme*.

KEYWORD GROUPING THEMES

Your keyword mix on Amazon will play many roles within your brand's conversion funnel, as shown in Figure 8–2 below. This is why we like to organize keywords into three main themes (brand, category, and competitor), as discussed in Chapter 6. These keywords will be vital to your new customer acquisition strategy as they can boost product discoverability for low-intent shoppers who don't have their hearts set on a certain brand when initially searching for a product.

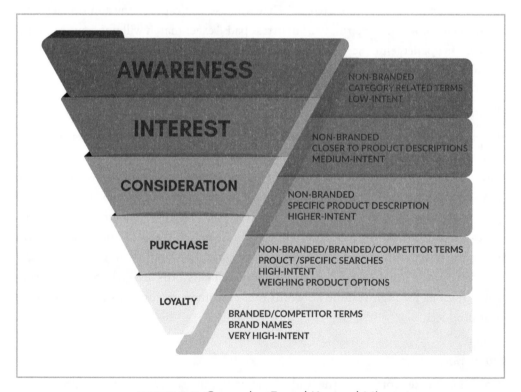

FIGURE 8–2. Conversion Funnel Keyword Mix

Brand Keywords

Brand keyword-driven traffic is important to lock down and defend from competitors early on in your advertising efforts. Someone who is searching your brand name on Amazon obviously has high intent to purchase one or more of your products. But as with many marketplaces, they can easily change their mind if another brand gets an opportunity to showcase their product—especially if that product is price- and review-competitive. That's why locking down your brand keyword space is so vital; direct competitors may be bidding on your brand terms to take away volume and market share from you.

Category Keywords

Category keywords are neither a defensive nor offensive tactic; category-level keywords (more fully described in Chapter 6) are purely for revenue growth and new customer acquisition. If you sell laundry detergent, it really doesn't matter much that your company owns the number-one brand in the world if Amazon shoppers are primarily searching for "laundry detergent" instead of "[your brand name] laundry detergent." There are approximately 250 new consumers born every minute around the world, and eventually, it will be time to introduce some of them to your wonderful brand.

Competitor Keywords

In the same way that brand keywords are a *defensive* advertising tactic, competitor keywords can be deployed as an *offensive* tool. Advertising on competitor terms is a great way to gauge the strength of a direct competitor's ad strategy. If you can consistently convert on a competitor's term, they probably aren't defending their brand search space as well as you are. Out of the three keyword themes, competitor keywords tend to be the least profitable upfront, but they can have a strong long-term payoff from a customer acquisition and market-share standpoint.

KEYWORD RESEARCH STRATEGY

Having a robust and refined keyword strategy will not only boost your advertising performance but will also pay dividends for your organic rankings. Amazon's complex search engine algorithm serves up products organically on the search results page based on a number of factors, including whether a product has an established history of converting on a specific search term. Since Amazon wants to serve up the most relevant and high-converting search results, a product that has established conversion rates will be preferred. Simply put, by driving conversions through your advertised keywords, you are boosting your organic ranking and sales.

The first step toward establishing a successful keyword strategy is conducting keyword research. This process is integral to keeping your ads relevant and competitive in the marketplace. Due to the ever-changing nature of how customers search for products, keyword research is an iterative process that you should revisit regularly during your campaigns.

Keyword Research Tools

A quick Google search for "Amazon keyword research tool" will return an overwhelming number of options for both free and subscription-based tools for keyword research. Most of them tend to have one thing in common, however: They aren't very helpful.

Though some of these tools may help reinforce the most obvious keywords for your product or category, they will most likely not unlock any new insights about what people are searching to find your product or similar products.

Out of all the free tools we have tested in-house, the only one we can readily recommend for its consistent results is Sonar (http://sonar-tool.com/us). Using this tool in combination with our other initial keyword research strategies should give your Amazon advertising strategy a solid foundation of terms with which to drive traffic.

Getting Granular with Keywords

If you want to find your most profitable keywords, you will need to dig into the data and get granular. The common keywords that most directly describe your product or its greater product category will most likely be expensive to gain visibility on. That's not to say that you shouldn't bid on them—especially if you are in a niche product category—but you shouldn't expect an exceptionally strong return. Your most profitable keywords will be on higher levels of granularity, whether that's a size qualifier ("mattress protector" vs. "*queen* mattress protector") or a product feature ("mattress protector" vs. "*waterproof* mattress protector").

Using the Amazon Search Bar for Keyword Research

Some of the most valuable resources for keyword research are hiding in plain sight on Amazon's search results page. Many established sellers on Amazon have packed their product titles and listings chock-full of high-converting keywords to ensure the site's algorithm will list their product within its organic search rankings. This can provide a wealth of information for advertisers just starting out on Amazon.

Try conducting a search on Amazon using your most basic and direct search term to find your (and your competitors') products. Copy the product titles from the first page or two of results and dump them into a text analysis tool such as Countwordsfree (https://countwordsfree.com) that will identify popular terms and phrases in the text. You now have a breakdown of the terms and product descriptors your competition has deemed high-converting. You can conduct the same process for product page descriptions as well. This is a useful analysis to perform when building an initial list of keywords to test.

Amazon's search bar is also a great jumping-off point for keyword research. Like most search engines, Amazon's search bar populates suggested terms once you've begun to type. The suggestions listed are the most popular variations of the keyword you initially typed. For example, if you type "earbud headphones" into the search bar, Amazon may suggest "earbud headphones with microphone," a longer keyword that could convert higher than the more general "earbud headphones." You can find even more keyword opportunities through the search bar by typing a general keyword, placing your cursor back at the beginning, and then typing a series of random letters. This will reveal a list of suggestions of search terms that have words *before* the keyword you typed. For example, if you type "earbud headphones" and follow the steps above, you will see suggestions such as "wireless earbud headphones" or "marshmallow earbud headphones." These suggestions change over time with shifts in consumer term usage and product appeal, so this is a simple process to check if there are any gaps in your keyword strategy.

These initial research and discovery tactics are a good way to build your keyword inventory from the ground up. Once you've created an initial list of keywords to bid and advertise on, you're ready to move on to the next step.

YOUR KEYWORD ORGANIZATION PLAN

Before adding these keywords to your campaigns, you need to formulate a system that allows you to securely store these keywords, sort them by product category, and determine a strategic product mix for keywords based on your business goals. The more systematic and efficient this process is, the easier it is to scale when your keyword list begins to grow ever larger.

In summary, sort your new keywords, determine a strategy and goals through which they will be measured, and then add them to your campaigns. After this, you'll find the most significant keyword insights will come from the search terms and conversion data that begins to flow through your newly optimized campaigns. We will dive into this topic in much more detail as it is a cornerstone for maintaining your Sponsored Products campaigns.

As mentioned before, categorizing your keywords by traffic type (brand, category, and competitor) is a great way to ensure clear profitability metrics for each type. Within these traffic categories, breaking your keywords down another level by *product category* adds a new strategic dimension. Now the levers you will use to adjust your advertising campaigns are coming into view. For each product category within your catalog, you have highly relevant keywords that cover each traffic type. You can read more about keyword strategies within campaign structures in Chapter 10.

In late 2018, Amazon released a new feature called portfolios which allow you to more easily manage your campaigns within the interface. One of the main benefits of portfolios is the ability to group campaigns together based on their product category, traffic type, brand, or any other way that interests you. You also have the ability to set portfolio level budget caps. This can be especially helpful if you know that you want to dedicate a certain percentage of your overall budget to a specific strategy or brand. By using portfolios, you can quickly view performance trends at the portfolio level.

Outside of campaign monitoring and management, portfolios also offer a few other unique benefits including the integration with billing statements, ability to manage multiple stores from one account, and access to multiple accounts from a single login. One important thing to note with portfolios is that a single campaign can only belong to one portfolio, so be sure to consider this before utilizing multiple strategies to assign portfolios.

Now that we have discussed the methods to formulate an effective advertising strategy for not only your product catalog but also your traffic segments, keyword mix, and product category priorities, in the next part of the book we will move into the structural best practices that are the best vehicle for these strategies to begin producing results.

Chapter 9

Campaign Structure

Mission defines strategy, and strategy defines structure.

—Peter Drucker, Austrian-American management consultant (1909–2005)

When something goes wrong in business, the natural tendency is to blame someone; it's a "people" problem. And while there are definitely "people" problems, my experience in business has taught me to step back and look at the problem to see if it can be solved with a different process, technology, or structure.

Of course, it could be you've got the wrong person in a role, but if a problem happens again and again, with multiple people? The answer, of course, is to establish a structure or process that creates success again and again.

In this chapter, I'll outline the importance of having a solid structure for your Amazon ad campaigns as well as where to go to build your campaigns.

BUILDING THE RIGHT STRUCTURE

The brutal truth about building a digital campaign structure, including but not limited to Amazon, is that the work required to create a great (i.e., highly structured) one is unglamorous, detailed, and (for brands with thousands of SKUs) very time-consuming.

It's also true that to get the maximum scale, control, and profitability out of your Amazon ad campaigns, you absolutely have to build a strong structure.

You need a campaign structure in place that mirrors your objectives, which you read about in Chapter 6. By building a smart campaign structure, you'll have control over the progress you're making, be better able to apply bids based on profit and growth objectives, and therefore have an easier way to measure and scale your campaign.

No "Easy Button"

There will always be vendors offering tools to the digital advertising ecosystem, and their implicit or explicit promise is usually, "Buy this tool and it's as good as hitting the 'easy button.' Everything just works beautifully once this is in place." It's typical for a digital ad tool to offer bid optimization, targeting control, repricing, or reporting, but in my 16 years of digital marketing experience, I haven't seen one that magically altered your campaign structure with the push of a button (or created a smart one based on your unique business goals).

The problem with this promise is that if no one ever properly builds your Amazon campaign structure, all you'll have is a questionably optimized digital ad campaign balanced on top of a poorly organized structure. It's like optimizing a rowboat by adding better oars instead of simply upgrading to a powerboat with a 225 hp motor. The powerboat will get you across the lake faster, no matter how good those oars are.

If you already have your Amazon ad campaign structure in place as you read this—either because you set it up initially yourself or because you inherited it from someone else—it's likely that after reading this part of the book you'll want to restructure them.

If you have not yet built your campaign structure, you're in the right place! You have a unique opportunity to build something really great from the ground up. If that's you, in the next section you'll see where to begin: Vendor Central or Seller Central.

VENDOR CENTRAL VS. SELLER CENTRAL: WHERE TO GO TO BUILD YOUR CAMPAIGNS

Do you sell *to* Amazon or sell *on* Amazon? Or do you do both? Once you know the answer to that question, you'll know where in the Amazon Advertising interface to start building your ad campaign structure. And once you know that, I'll outline how to begin building campaigns that help you gain new customers and grow your brand's momentum and revenue.

I've already briefly mentioned Vendor Central and Seller Central, but let's unpack the two options in terms of campaign building.

Vendor Central

If you sell *to* Amazon, you'll want to get started in Vendor Central. Selling to Amazon is generally an invitation-only wholesale program made to large brand manufacturers (many with their own factories) or very strong distributors. When your company registers as a vendor, Amazon becomes a full-time seller of your products in the same way as Target or Walmart might.

Like Target or Walmart, when you sell to Amazon, they buy and store inventory they've purchased from you (which you ship to their various warehouses); they then manage everything from shipping to pricing to customer service to returns. So it's a standard wholesale model where you negotiate price and terms upfront and Amazon bears the costs and risks of selling to their customers.

If you do sell to Amazon, you'll get access to the Amazon Advertising console from within your Vendor Central account; this is where you'll build your ad campaigns.

As a vendor to Amazon, you'll also get access to premium marketing opportunities, such as A+ Detail Pages (more detailed product listings, larger images, comparison charts, videos, and more) and Amazon Vine (a program where top Amazon reviewers can test your products and write reviews about them even before your products arrive at Amazon's warehouses).

Seller Central

If you want to sell *on* Amazon (i.e., on the Amazon marketplace), you'll begin using your Seller Central account to access the "Advertising" link at the top menu bar, which is where you'll begin building your ad campaigns.

Selling on the Amazon marketplace also gets you access to additional marketing opportunities. For example, if you own the trademark for the brand name that appears on your products and you apply for Amazon Brand Registry, you can create Enhanced Brand Content (EBC) product descriptions and control most detail page content on your brand's products. In addition, you can enroll in the Amazon Early Reviewer Program. With this program, Amazon will help you get up to five reviews from customers who have already purchased your product by giving them a small reward (such as a $3 gift card) in exchange for providing feedback.

AD PROGRAMS ON AMAZON

Now that you know where to begin, here's what advertising programs are available to vendors and sellers on Amazon. Recently, Amazon launched a portal for advertising, appropriately called "Amazon Advertising." From the site (https://advertising.amazon. com), you can register or sign in to access advertising within Seller Central or the Advertising console (for vendors, this was formerly known as Amazon Marketing Services).

As you can see in Figure 9–1, while you access the advertising in different places depending on whether you're a vendor or a seller, two of the three Amazon ad formats

FIGURE 9–1. Available Ad Programs for Vendors and Sellers

(Sponsored Products and Sponsored Brands) are available in both places. Let's look at each of them now.

Sponsored Products

Sponsored Products ads are triggered by customer searches on Amazon so you can reach customers looking for products like yours. These ads appear in the search results and on product detail pages. When a shopper clicks on your ad, they're taken directly to your product detail page. You (somewhat) control the experience in the shopper's journey because you choose which products to advertise, assign keywords to those products, and enter a cost-per-click bid. You pay only when a shopper clicks on your ad, much like Google Ads.

Sponsored Products are available with two targeting methods: automatic and manual. With automatic targeting, an Amazon algorithm will collect and use highly relevant keywords for all chosen products, typically based on the context of your product page. With manual targeting, you specifically choose the keywords to match your products with ads. This ad type shows up below Sponsored Brands but above the organic rankings, as shown in Figure 9–2 below.

FIGURE 9–2. Sponsored Products

Sponsored Brands

Sponsored Brands ads are also triggered by customer searches on Amazon, but they may appear at the top of a page on desktop and mobile platforms and feature up to three products of your choice along with your logo and your customized ad copy, as shown in Figure 9–3 below. These often appear at the top of the first page in search results on Amazon and drive traffic to a custom landing page or Amazon Store if a shopper clicks on the ad itself. Clicking on one of the three featured products will take the shopper directly to the respective product detail page. You must be enrolled in the Amazon Brand Registry to create and run these ads.

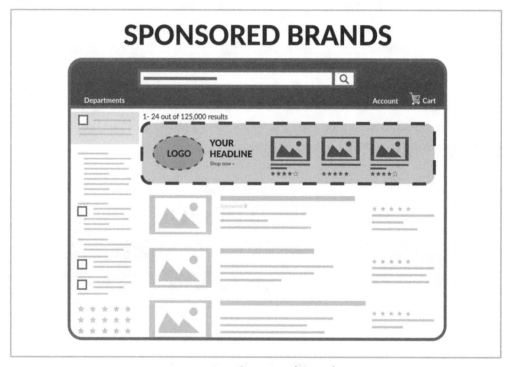

FIGURE 9–3. Sponsored Brands

FOR AMAZON VENDORS ONLY: PRODUCT DISPLAY ADS

Product Display ads, available only to vendors who sell to Amazon, are cost-per-click product or interest-targeted display ads that drive shoppers to your product detail pages. They are used to deliver highly relevant ads to shoppers with specific interests (including category interest) or to shoppers who are actively viewing specific products.

Product Display ads are shown in a variety of places on the Amazon site, as seen in Figure 9–4 on page 71, including:

FIGURE 9–4. Product Display Ads

- On the product detail page below product info (desktop and mobile)
- On the "read all reviews" page
- At the very top of the offer listing page
- In Amazon-generated emails (such as follow-ups and recommendation emails)

SHOWCASE YOUR BRAND WITH AN AMAZON STORE

If you want to direct traffic from your Sponsored Brands ads to an Amazon Store, you'll obviously need to create one if your brand doesn't have one yet. Building an Amazon Store helps drive shopper engagement with a customized destination to help customers learn more about your brand. This is a free, self-service option that was introduced in 2017, and Amazon has been releasing new features and capabilities since its launch.

We often tell our clients that it's a no-brainer when it comes to having an Amazon Store for their brand. The main benefits of an Amazon Store include:

- Ease of creation and use
- A multipage experience for shoppers to learn more about your brand and products
- Integrated promotional features

Let's now take a deeper look at each of these benefits.

Ease of Creation

Amazon has made it fairly simple for companies to create an Amazon Store for their brands with pre-designed templates and an easy-to-navigate interface. Although it may sound daunting, no coding or site-design skills are needed to launch an Amazon Store. To create your store, use the store builder in the Amazon interface. As you can see in Figure 9–5 below, you can get to the store builder within Vendor Central by clicking on the "Stores" link at the top of the Amazon Advertising interface.

FIGURE 9–5. Accessing the Store Builder

The store builder allows you to choose from pre-designed templates and then customize your design using tiles. Start by creating your main page and then create additional pages to expand on your different product categories.

Almost all of this can be done through the self-service portal. One thing that can't, however, is the ability to shorten your store's URL. A shortened URL makes it easier for customers to find your store, especially for shoppers who are familiar with your brand and want to go to your store directly without having to click through Amazon to get there. It can also be useful for marketing materials, since it is short, simple, and easy to remember. Once you have your Amazon Store up and running, ask your Amazon representative to help you with this.

A Multipage, Brand-Centered Shopping Experience

Shoppers can navigate to your Amazon Store from your brand name, which appears as a link on product detail pages. You can also send traffic to your store from Sponsored Brands campaigns or ads from other sources (e.g., Facebook ads).

Once a shopper lands on your Amazon Store, they can use the store's navigation tools such as the navigation bar to explore your content and learn more about your brand message, products, categories, promotions, etc. Use your main page to showcase top products and introduce your brand, and then use sub-pages to dig deeper into your products and categories. Since you get to design the store, you control what shoppers see, where they see it, and how it is positioned. This level of control and creativity allows you to create a brand-centered shopping experience.

If you already have marketing materials (images, videos, descriptive images, etc.) that you have used on other platforms, you can save yourself some time and energy by using these same assets on your Amazon Store.

Integrated Promotional Feature

One major benefit of Amazon Stores is that you can send traffic from Sponsored Brands and other channels (such as Facebook) to your store. This is a great opportunity if you're using Sponsored Brands to generate awareness for your products because when a shopper clicks on those ads, they will be directed to a store that is custom-built around your brand's story. Additionally, you can drive traffic to your Amazon Store from other channels through your store's URL (e.g., by including it in a blog or social media post).

Amazon Stores also include links that allow shoppers to organically share your Amazon Store on their social media accounts. This feature includes the ability to share

PERRY ELLIS INTERNATIONAL

After a successful Prime Day in 2017, Perry Ellis International (a leading fashion brand for men and women) began to analyze their ad data and concluded that although they had driven a high volume of sales, they could probably be achieving more profitable conversions at their current rate of spend.

Michelle Reed, senior VP at Perry Ellis, expressed the major concerns they faced with Amazon Advertising: "There was a bandwidth issue and an expertise issue," she told me. "Under our umbrella, we had nine or ten brands and businesses that were managed by different people. They were fragmented and all over the place. There really was no optimizing."

Additionally, they were approaching the end of their fiscal year and had a lofty goal of increasing their return on ad spend (ROAS) to $10 while concurrently facing limited budgets for their upcoming holiday season. Recounting these daunting hurdles, Reed said: "The ROAS completely dipped, and we had to cut off one brand entirely because they had reached their budget and there was still time left in the year."

PERRY ELLIS INTERNATIONAL, continued

Acknowledging a solid plan of action was necessary, Michelle reached out to my company for help in October 2017.

Evan Davis, our marketplaces strategist at ROI Revolution, developed a game plan for the account: "We worked closely with Michelle to determine how to use the remaining budget most effectively," he said. "We then focused on the core products that were really going to maximize sales and expanded campaign coverage in areas that would make the biggest impact."

"Having the trust that ROI Revolution is managing the budget, optimizing, and knowing what goals and strategies are priorities was a big piece," Reed said. "The reporting was really critical because I think without it, it's just your gut and your estimate, but the numbers are the numbers."

Our team was also able to recover account history, creating the analysis and reporting that allowed Perry Ellis to really understand the significance of their historical data. "We're [now] able to look at this year over last year, or month over month; to me that was a critical miss that immediately we were able to see benefits from," Reed said. "Our ROAS continues to be strong. We are very pleased with the payoff of the campaigns."

By December, Perry Ellis had the account back under budget and had exceeded their target return by more than 30 percent.

on social platforms like Facebook, Twitter, and Pinterest. These social sharing buttons allow shoppers to tell their friends or followers about a brand they have found on Amazon that they really love.

Another key benefit is the ability to feature active promotions on your store. If your brand has any active promotions, you can add a widget to your store that will automatically showcase those products on your store. This is a great opportunity to increase the visibility of these deals, especially if you place the deals widget on the main page of your Amazon Store. This feature is especially useful during periods of high seasonality, as this is a great time to feature any active deals on Amazon.

For example, if your brand has promotions or deals running for Cyber Monday and another round of deals running for the first week of December, this widget will automatically populate with the available deals for each round of promotions. You can easily add or remove this widget on your Amazon Store and then resubmit to see the change.

Now that we have introduced each ad format and their respective qualities and uses, we will take a much more detailed look at how to get started with these formats for your advertising efforts. We will cover the nuances of each ad format and their variations for sellers vs. vendors and how they can be leveraged to drive profitable growth for your brand.

Let's get started in our next chapter by building your first ad in Amazon's most popular ad format, Sponsored Products.

Chapter 10

Getting Started with Sponsored Products

Today, online commerce saves customers money and precious time. Tomorrow, through personalization, online commerce will accelerate the very process of discovery.

—Jeff Bezos, letter to Amazon shareholders (1997 annual report)

Sponsored Products are a great place to begin when you're just getting started with advertising on Amazon. You can run automatic campaigns by simply selecting your products and setting the appropriate bids and budgets. Then you can use the data you amass from those automatic campaigns to build your manual campaigns.

Because all Amazon merchants (or vendors) can run Sponsored Products ads, the format is the most popular form of advertising on the site, accounting for an estimated 82 percent of all Amazon ad spending (Q3, 2017), according to ad agency Merkle.

Sponsored Products deliver the highest sales per click of any Amazon advertising channel. So it's not just the multiple placements and high conversion rates that make this an enticing opportunity; it's the superior results of the ad format as well. There is plenty of opportunity to drive growth at an acceptable cost using Amazon Sponsored Products.

National Marker Company (NMC), a client of ours which manufactures safety identification products, was facing an industry in flux; the competitive landscape was headed more and more toward digital advertising, and they needed to make some aggressive moves to stay ahead. Amazon was the battleground that needed to be won, but they weren't sure where to begin.

Derek Falardeau, NMC's ecommerce manager, knew there were a few hurdles right out of the gate; they're a smaller company, and budgets needed to stay within the guidelines. Additionally, they had a fairly narrow ACoS goal of 10 to 15 percent, which didn't leave a lot of room for experimentation.

In late July 2017, my team went to work on their Amazon marketing efforts. We quickly structured NMC's campaign for Amazon and got to work building granular Sponsored Products ads for all NMC products, ensuring coverage for every product in their catalog.

The change in traffic was almost immediate. NMC began to see revenue growth nearly every month. Even during a period that was historically known as the company's slow season, they were now experiencing steady growth. Falardeau told me, "Our

BUY BOX CONSIDERATIONS

Whether on the search results page or product detail pages, your ads are only eligible to appear when you are winning the buy box. When, as a seller, you "win" the buy box, it means that you are the seller Amazon chooses to fill that order for that customer.

While this normally won't be a factor for brands or sellers who have exclusivity for the products they sell, other sellers in the Amazon marketplace will face greater obstacles toward achieving a high buy box win percentage (the number of times they win the buy box vs. other sellers). Additionally, even if your brand holds Brand Registry exclusivity, you could still lose the buy box if your pricing is drastically higher than that of other sellers.

Keep in mind, advertising impressions increase your at-bats, which in turn increases the raw number of times you win the buy box compared with organic traffic from Amazon alone. This increase in sales will also affect your seller history, which could increase your overall buy box percentage even from organic traffic.

traditional slow season for our distributors didn't reflect on Amazon." They had found the silver bullet that pierced the "seasonality" barrier.

ROI Revolution Marketplaces Strategist Ben Smith said, "Sponsored Products ads were absolutely essential for NMC's growth this last year. They only had a couple of campaigns active when we jumped in, so we hit the ground running on buildouts. Within the first week of August, we had built 30 campaigns, and within the first month there were close to 60 active campaigns. Along the way, a lot of new product opportunities that were not top of mind for NMC were discovered, and we were able to exploit those new, profitable areas to keep momentum going."

When asked about the overall impact of adding a strong Amazon campaign strategy to their branding efforts, Falardeau said, "The revenue increased, and it directly correlated to not only our advertising sales but our sales in our main account as well."

When NMC started out, Falardeau said that Amazon was a relatively small driver of their overall revenue. "After roughly a year and a half," he stated, "Amazon has become a much larger contributor to NMC's total revenue package for the upcoming business year."

If you want sales growth at an acceptable cost, create your first campaigns using Sponsored Products. Let's get started by creating some automatic Sponsored Products campaigns.

AUTOMATIC SPONSORED PRODUCTS CAMPAIGNS

The easiest way to get started and cover all your SKUs is by using automatic Sponsored Products ad campaigns. Automatic Sponsored Products campaigns enable you to target all relevant customer searches based on your product listing information. Such campaigns allow your product ads to display on a far wider range of search queries than would be available through manual targeting.

These campaigns are perfect for newcomers to Amazon. They are easy to implement and an excellent way to develop a baseline of data on product and advertising performance. They will also allow you to build a relevant keyword library as a basis for future, more laser-targeted manual campaigns.

In late 2018, Amazon made significant updates to its automatic campaign targeting capabilities. Now advertisers can bid on four separate targeting methods to further improve ad granularity and return. Two of the methods focus on the targeting of customer searches, while the other two focus on product page views.

- *Close match*—this targeting method allows the algorithm to place your product in customer searches for products highly related to your product

- *Loose match*—this targeting method allows the algorithm to place your product in customer searches for products only loosely related to your product
- *Complements*—this targeting method allows the algorithm to place your ad on product pages for products that complement your advertised product
- *Substitute*—this targeting method allows the algorithm to place your ad on product pages for products for which your advertised product may be a direct substitute

Before you get started with automatic campaigns, determine which products you want to advertise. Do you want to advertise your entire line or just certain categories of products? Feel free to reread the section in Chapter 6, "Determine Your Objectives for the Quarter," for a refresher if necessary. Also determine how much you want to spend each day on advertising so you can set your per-click bid and daily budget.

Now let's dive into how to create them.

Automatic Sponsored Products Campaigns for Sellers

If you are a vendor to Amazon, feel free to skip to the next section of this chapter where I will walk you through the steps of launching an automatic Sponsored Products campaign in Vendor Central. Otherwise, continue reading for the details on launching an automatic Sponsored Products campaign in Seller Central.

In Seller Central, you will want to center your automatic Sponsored Products campaigns on product categories. By grouping similar products together, you will be able to set bids and budgets appropriately for each category. Each product category will have an automatic Sponsored Products campaign with the respective products included in an ad group within that campaign.

For example, let's say you sell children's apparel and you are just getting started with Amazon Advertising. You may want to consider launching automatic Sponsored Products campaigns for each of the following product categories: toddler shirts, toddler pants, toddler dresses, toddler shorts, etc. The toddler shirts automatic Sponsored Products campaign will have one ad group that includes all your toddler shirt products.

CASE STUDY: BRONDELL INC.

One of our newer clients was Brondell Inc., a San Francisco manufacturer of Japanese-inspired bidet products, water filtration, and air purification systems. They wanted to grow their revenue with Amazon and asked for help after hearing about my team from a consultant.

CASE STUDY: BRONDELL INC., continued

Brondell had seen some early success in their industry, earning numerous awards and helping their brand stay at the top of the competitive landscape. But as is always the case over time, the tide eventually began to turn. With more competition sprouting up every year, being first to market was no longer giving them the edge they had once enjoyed. The problem was not competitors with better-quality products; it was competitors with more extensive advertising coverage for their products.

Brondell Sales Account Manager Matt Groom knew they needed to expand their advertising, but he also knew a scattershot approach could prove costly. "We wanted to ramp up the ads quickly, but there was a lot of risk," he said. "We thought that money could be spent really frivolously on a trial-and-error basis, and we didn't want to waste any more money figuring things out."

After being tapped to manage Brondell's Amazon efforts, we identified automatic campaigns as one of the simplest ways to increase product coverage and market insight for the company. My team's Marketplaces Strategist Grayson Cross said, "The first thing we did within the account was to ensure that all products were included in auto campaigns. This was a crucial effort sorely missing from their previous strategy, so we got to work building out auto campaigns immediately."

After the first four months of managing Brondell's account, investment in automatic campaigns eventually became 33 percent of their total Sponsored Products spend. As a result, Groom pointed out, the account saw an increase in revenue and a lower advertising cost of sale while still remaining within budget. "Revenue was increasing dramatically over spend," Groom said. "Normally, we see a dip in sales in March, April, May, June, July, and August, but we were actually growing revenue not only month over month, but year over year."

"I wouldn't underestimate automatic campaigns just because they are easy to set up," Cross said. "They're extremely valuable, both for their ability to discover new keywords you haven't thought to target yet and for collecting data that allows you to build out deliberate, highly granular manual campaigns down the road. It takes a lot of risk out of the equation when scaling, so we always recommend running them."

If you already have experience with advertising on Amazon and are looking for a more granular approach, you might want to consider breaking out each product into its own ad group within the campaign. The campaign would still be centered on the product category, but rather than having only one ad group with all relevant products, each product would be in its own ad group. This approach allows greater control over the bids of each product.

Once you determine which products you would like to advertise, as well as your per-click bids and budgets, you can get started with launching your automatic Sponsored Products campaign.

To get started in Seller Central, go to the "Advertising" link at the top of the page and then click on "Campaign Manager." Follow the ten steps outlined below to get your automatic campaign up and running:

1. Click on "Create Campaign."
2. Select "Sponsored Products" as the campaign type as shown in Figure 10–1 below.

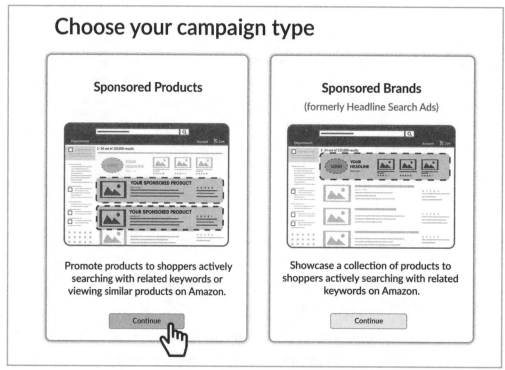

FIGURE 10–1. Choosing a Campaign Type

3. Give your campaign a name. Choose a name that indicates the product category (e.g., Holiday Favorites—Automatic Campaign, as seen in Figure 10–2 on page 83).

FIGURE 10–2. Choose a Campaign Name

4. Select the time frame over which you would like the campaign to run. We recommend selecting "No End Date" unless there is a specific reason the campaign should end at a certain time (e.g., campaigns related to holidays). You can always select a specific end date at another time or pause or terminate the campaign at any time.

5. Fill in the daily budget you are willing to spend on this campaign. You can adjust the daily budget after the campaign has launched as well.

6. Choose "Automatic Targeting" as the targeting type.

7. Give your first ad group a name. If you plan on only having one ad group for all products, this will be the only group you need to launch. If you want multiple ad groups (e.g., a separate ad group for each product), you can launch these additional groups after the campaign has launched.

8. Search for the products you want to include in this ad group. You can search by product name, SKU, or ASIN.

9. Once you have selected all the products you want to include, set the default bid for the ad group. This will apply to all products in that group.

10. Finally, click "Launch Campaign" to launch your automatic Sponsored Products campaign.

As a reminder, if you are taking a more granular approach to your automatic Sponsored Products campaigns, you will need to launch additional ad groups for products that were not included in the initial ad group.

Automatic Sponsored Products Campaigns for Vendors

If you are selling to Amazon through Vendor Central, the process of launching an automatic Sponsored Products campaign is very similar to the one used in Seller Central. The primary difference is that there are no ad groups, so unlike on Seller Central, you do not have the option to separate each product into its own ad group. Other than that, your approach will be the same in setting up automatic campaigns, although the step-by-step instructions will vary given the different interfaces.

To get started with Amazon Advertising through Vendor Central, log in to your advertising account (https://advertising.amazon.com) and then select "Advertising Console." Follow the nine steps outlined below to get your automatic Sponsored Products campaign up and running:

1. Click on "Create Campaign."

2. Choose "Sponsored Products" as the campaign type. See Figure 10–3 on page 85.

3. Give your campaign a name that indicates the product category (e.g., Toddler Shirts—Automatic Campaign). See Figure 10–4 on page 85.

4. Choose the duration of the campaign. We recommend setting the campaign to run continuously beginning that day unless there is a specific reason the campaign should end at a certain time (e.g., campaigns related to holidays).

5. Fill in the daily budget you are willing to spend on this campaign. You can adjust the daily budget after the campaign has launched as well.

6. Select "Automatic Targeting" as the targeting type.

7. Search for the products you want to include in this campaign. You can search by product name or ASIN. Continue searching for and adding products until all the desired products are selected.

8. Set the per-click bid you are willing to pay. This bid will apply to all products included in the campaign.

9. Click "Launch Campaign."

Once your automatic Sponsored Products campaigns are built and running, you'll want to wait a couple of weeks for the data to start pouring in. Automatic campaigns

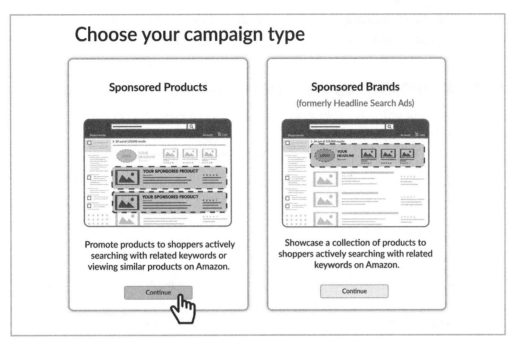

FIGURE 10–3. Choose Your Campaign Type

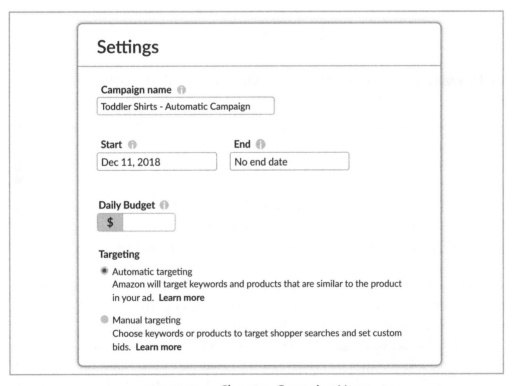

FIGURE 10–4. Choose a Campaign Name

will begin to shed light on which of your products have great volume, which keywords drive strong traffic, and what your initial profitability looks like.

MANUAL SPONSORED PRODUCTS CAMPAIGNS

The next step will be to create another set of Sponsored Products campaigns where the structure is built manually.

Here's why you want to build manual Sponsored Products campaigns:

■ Manual campaigns allow you to increase your bid on specific keywords or groups of keywords that perform well for more precise targeting, which can lead to more sales.

■ You can add phrase and exact match targeting, which allow you to bid higher on more precise keyword targets.

■ Manual campaigns allow you to bid in a granular way for maximum profitability by making it easier to bid down or pause underperforming keywords.

■ Have a keyword theme you want to test? You can do that with manual campaigns.

Manual Sponsored Products campaigns offer just what they imply: more precise decision making from sellers. You must manually set the keywords for these campaigns, which means they require more initial work to get them up and running, but in return, they give you a more refined and targeted level of control.

IMPLEMENTING A MANUAL CAMPAIGN STRUCTURE

Taking the manual approach can seem overwhelming at first, especially if you're working with several different consumer goods categories, which is why some people never go that route. But if you need to reduce wasteful spending in the short term and get visible results in the near future, rolling out a manual campaign structure can be an absolute necessity.

One of my clients recently found themselves struggling to internally manage their Amazon campaigns; these campaigns were broken out by respective categories, but without the proper attention to detail, they were essentially bleeding money.

The client came to my team for assistance with their Amazon efforts, and our in-depth keyword research uncovered some terms that were spending consistently and seemed relevant but were not actually driving sales. This was the root of the issue, and the solution was an in-depth manual restructuring.

We first located which search queries were good keyword opportunities based on their revenue and profitability. Then we used tiered bids to be more aggressive with exact match targeting and used considerably lower bids for broader keywords to keep costs in check. Further, we strategically eliminated wasted spend by layering on negative keywords, which allowed us to better funnel queries to the areas that had proved to result in profitable conversions.

After implementing this manual campaign structure, our client saw a 55-percent increase in revenue and a 4-percent decrease in ad cost within their first month of management.

The work required to implement this structure is time-consuming and somewhat intense but so is the payoff. Don't shirk your responsibility to build these campaigns just because they seem like a lot of work.

We will take a deeper dive into the best practices of manual campaigns, but for now, let's start at the beginning and learn when is the best time to set up a manual campaign.

Timing Considerations for Manual Campaign Building

Manual campaigns are ideal once you've had a chance to analyze the product and keyword data from your automatic campaigns. Manual campaigns give you the opportunity to bid more aggressively on the terms that are more likely to convert for the products you choose to advertise. This allows you to focus on optimal profitability and weed out underperforming terms.

As with automatic campaigns, start by determining your daily ad budget and which products you want to advertise.

STRUCTURE MANUAL SPONSORED PRODUCTS CAMPAIGNS BY KEYWORD THEME

Manual Sponsored Products campaigns allow you to run a tightly structured ad campaign. I have seen a variety of strategies suggested as the best way to structure manual campaigns. After more than three years of running manual Sponsored Products campaigns in Seller Central and Vendor Central, I have found what I believe to be the optimal structure: keyword-themed manual campaigns.

Whereas automatic campaigns are structured by product category, I recommend structuring your manual campaigns by keyword theme. This structure has two main advantages:

1. *You can avoid keyword duplication.* We often speak with brand owners who struggle to manage keywords and bids across their accounts, especially when their manual campaigns are well-established and include hundreds or thousands of keywords. It can be tempting to structure your manual campaigns by product, but this can dupli-cate keywords across multiple campaigns and ad groups, leading to unmanageable keywords and bids. Another issue that comes with keyword duplication is split

traffic. Multiple iterations of the same keyword are essentially fighting for the same placements. Although duplicate keywords within the same account will not inflate the per-click bid, they can still split the traffic and make account management much more difficult than it has to be.

2. *You have a clear picture of how profitable each keyword theme is and can make the necessary optimizations.* For example, if your brand sells kitchen appliances, you might have a manual campaign for category traffic targeting "toaster" keywords. In this example, "toaster" is the keyword theme and the campaign is targeting keywords in the toaster category. With this structure, you will know how much it costs to acquire a customer who is not loyal to a specific brand and is searching for a toaster. Profitability is going to vary by keyword theme and even more so by the traffic type that is being targeted (i.e., brand, category, or competitor). When brand and category keywords exist within the same campaign and ad group, it is nearly impossible to know your cost per acquisition on new customers vs. returning customers. Keyword-themed manual campaigns also allow you to funnel the appropriate amount of spend toward each theme, which in turn means you can allocate spend based on profitability to work toward your overall goal.

Before you can launch your first manual Sponsored Products campaign, you will need to decide on the keywords you would like to target. Using what you read in Chapter 8 about keyword research, create a list of keywords you want to target in your manual campaigns.

Then categorize these keywords according to theme. Group keywords together that share the same keyword theme and traffic type (category, brand, or competitor).

For example, if one of your category keyword themes is "toaster," you might have the following group of keywords for that theme: two slice toaster, stainless steel toaster, bread toaster, kitchen toaster, etc. You might also have a brand campaign and a competitor campaign for the same keyword theme, each with its own group of keywords.

GUIDELINES FOR SETTING BIDS IN MANUAL SPONSORED PRODUCTS CAMPAIGNS

You'll want each of these traffic types (brand, category, and competitor) to have different baseline bids.

You can expect to pay more for generic, category-level keywords that have high search volume. Brand and competitor keywords can vary in the cost-per-click bid required to win the placement, but each of these traffic types generally performs differently.

When adding new keywords, it can be helpful to think about the potential search volume and specificity of the keyword. *Head term keywords* are keywords that are competitive in nature due to their high search volume. Head terms are usually short, no longer than one or two words. The other type are *long tail keywords*, which are specific to your product and are made up of three- or four-word phrases.

Match Type Considerations in Setting Bids

You should add both types of keywords in all three match types (broad, phrase, and exact) to catch as much traction as possible. We talked about these match types in Chapter 8, but to refresh your memory, broad match keywords are the most inclusive; ads can show when the keyword is part of the shopper's search term (in any order) or a close variant of the keyword. Ads show for phrase match keywords when a shopper searches for the exact keyword, but they can include additional words before or after the keyword. Exact match is the most targeted keyword match type; ads only show for exact match keywords when a shopper searches for your exact keyword without any additional words included. You can also add negative phrase and exact match keywords to your campaigns after they begin running, which will be covered in Chapter 14. See Figure 10–5 below for a breakdown of the different traffic types associated with bid amount.

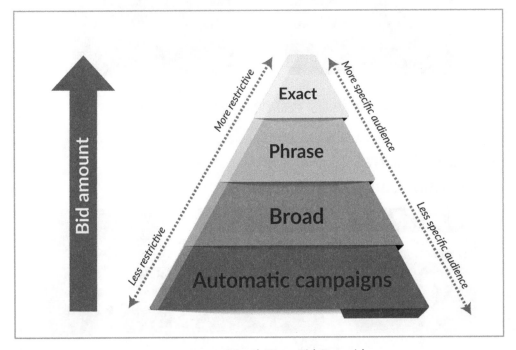

FIGURE 10–5. Match Type Bid Pyramid

Choose the Products You'll Advertise for Each Theme

Once you have your list of keywords categorized and bids chosen, you will need to decide which products to advertise for each keyword theme. Because we are taking a very granular approach with manual campaigns, you can choose a unique set of products for each ad group within Seller Central. For vendors, the products are associated at the campaign level (since ad groups are not available), and those products could appear for any of the keywords in that campaign. In both cases, this structure allows for optimal relevancy and proper keyword-product alignment.

Below, in Figures 10–6 and 10–7, you can see what the ideal manual campaign structure looks like in Vendor Central and Seller Central.

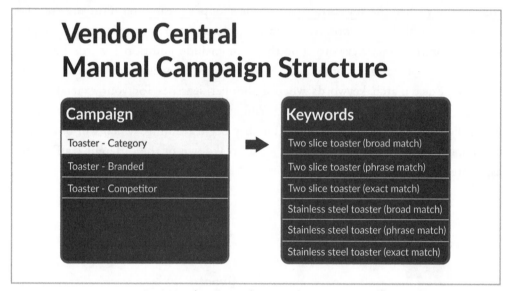

FIGURE 10–6. Vendor Central Manual Campaign Structure

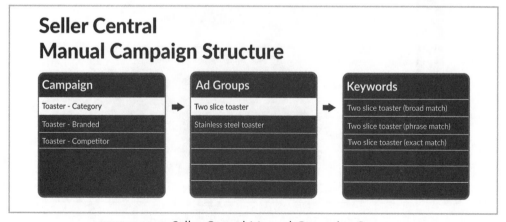

FIGURE 10–7. Seller Central Manual Campaign Structure

Now that you understand the reasoning behind our recommended structure for manual campaigns, it's time to start thinking about how to apply this structure to your account.

Manual Sponsored Products Campaigns for Sellers

To launch a manual campaign in Seller Central, go to the "Advertising" link at the top of the page and then click on Campaign Manager. Follow the 12 steps outlined below to get your campaign up and running.

1. Click on "Create Campaign."
2. Choose "Sponsored Products" as the campaign type. See Figure 10–8.

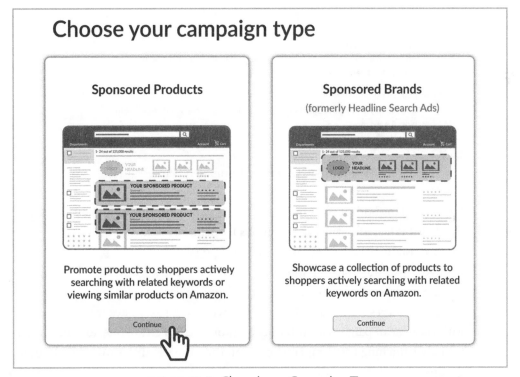

FIGURE 10–8. Choosing a Campaign Type

3. Give your campaign a name. Choose a name that indicates the keyword theme (e.g., Toaster–Category–Manual Campaign). See Figure 10–9 on page 92.
4. Select the time frame in which you would like the campaign to run. We recommend selecting "No End Date" unless there is a specific reason it should end at a certain time (e.g., campaigns related to holidays). You can always select an end date at another time or pause or terminate the campaign at any time.

FIGURE 10–9. Choose a Campaign Name

5. Fill in the daily budget you are willing to spend on this campaign. You can adjust the daily budget after the campaign has launched as well.

6. Choose "Manual Targeting" as the targeting type.

7. Give your first ad group a name, which should be the keyword that is being targeted. Since you will be creating an ad group for each keyword you would like to target and its respective match types, you will most likely have many ad groups within each campaign. You will only be prompted to create one ad group when initially launching the campaign, but you can go back afterward and add more groups.

8. Search for the products you want to include in this ad group by product name, SKU, or ASIN.

9. Once you have selected all the products you want to include, set the default bid for the ad group. This bid will apply to all keywords you add to this ad group. For this reason, you will want to adjust the bids once you have added the keywords to ensure that the keyword match types have tiered bids. Additionally, you can adjust bids by placement for top of search placements and/or product

detail page placements (see "Adjusting Sponsored Products Bids by Placement" on page 95, as well as a more detailed discussion in Chapter 15). This feature can be turned on or off at any time in the campaign settings.

10. When adding keywords, you can select keywords from a list of suggested keywords (based on the selected products) or add your own. If you are just starting out on Seller Central, it might be a good idea to look through the list of suggested keywords. Otherwise, we recommend using data from your automatic campaigns or other keyword research to choose the keywords for your manual campaigns.

11. Once all your keywords are selected and the appropriate bids are set, click "Launch Campaign."

12. To create additional ad groups for other keywords you want to include in this campaign, reopen the campaign and click "Create Ad Group." Repeat steps seven through ten for each additional ad group.

Amazon also allows you to make additions and changes to your campaign through a bulk upload option. Under the "Bulk Operations" link, you can download a bulk upload template, which you can use to make changes to the ad groups, keywords, products, etc.

Manual Sponsored Products Campaigns for Vendors

To launch a manual campaign through Vendor Central, go to the "Advertising" link at the top of the page and then click on "Campaign Manager." Follow the nine steps below to get your manual campaign up and running:

1. Click on "Create Campaign."

2. Choose "Sponsored Products" as the campaign type. See Figure 10–10 on page 94.

3. Give your campaign a name that indicates the product category (e.g., Toaster–Category–Manual Campaign). See Figure 10–11 on page 94.

4. Choose how long you would like the campaign to run. We recommend setting the campaign to run continuously beginning that day unless there is a specific reason it should end at a certain time.

5. Fill in the daily budget you are willing to spend on this campaign. You can adjust the budget after the campaign has been launched if needed.

6. Select "Manual Targeting" as the targeting type.

7. Search for the products you want to include in this campaign. You can search by product name or ASIN. Continue adding products until all of them have been selected.

8. Next add your keywords to the campaign. Remember, advertising campaigns in Vendor Central do not have ad groups, which means that all keywords

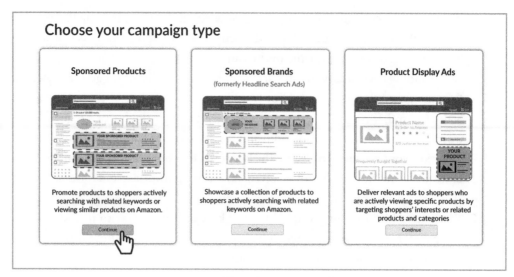

FIGURE 10–10. Choosing a Campaign Type

FIGURE 10–11. Choose a Campaign Name

should be relevant to all products within the campaign. You can choose from a list of suggested keywords, add your own keywords in the interface, or upload a spreadsheet of keywords. If you are just starting out on Vendor Central, it might be a good idea to look through the list of suggested keywords. Otherwise, we recommend using data from your automatic campaigns or other keyword research to choose keywords for your manual campaigns. If you are adding keywords in the interface, you can adjust the default bid for each one. Keep in mind the tiered bids for the keyword match types as you add them.

9. Now that you have added your products and keywords to your manual Sponsored Products campaign, click "Launch Campaign."

Product and Category Features for Manual Sponsored Products

In late 2018, Amazon also released a new feature within Manual Sponsored Products campaigns that allows advertisers to target individual products and product categories in addition to keywords. This development opens up numerous opportunities for advertisers to list their products against competitors on product pages and more broadly target a product category rather than a selection of keywords.

For product targeting, advertisers can now treat ASINs similarly to keywords by adding them to existing campaigns and ad groups and even adding negative ASIN targets similar to negative keywords. This will allow advertisers more control over where their ads are able to show on their own catalog's listings or competitor listings and can create a "blacklist" of listings they do not want visibility on via the negative targeting feature.

ADJUSTING SPONSORED PRODUCTS BIDS BY PLACEMENT

Amazon recently replaced what used to be known as Bid+ with the ability to adjust bids by placement. With this update, you can now set up to a 900 percent increase for either top-of-search placements on the first page or for product detail page placements. In the past, Bid+ was restricted to a 50 percent increase in bids for top-of-search placements. This update allows for more customization in the bidding strategy for Sponsored Products. Campaigns that were previously set up with Bid+ were automatically updated to increase bids by 50 percent for top of search placements, and the performance of those campaigns should not be impacted by the change.

With category targeting, advertisers can select from Amazon's preset categories and sub-categories and deploy Sponsored Products ads to users searching in these categories. These ads still show in the typical placements for Sponsored Products including search results and product pages. Advertisers can further filter category targeting by brand, price range, and review count. Targeting certain brands, products that fall within a comparable price range, or products with inferior reviews are all strategy options that you can now deploy with this updated form of targeting. These updated targeting methods are promising for ensuring that ads show to high-intent shoppers and increase visibility within search results and product pages for highly relevant products and brands.

Sponsored Products ads serve as the primary traffic engine for your advertising efforts on Amazon. With Sponsored Products, you can increase your visibility and targeting with highly granular keywords and ad groups. This strategic approach is great for achieving profitable, conversion-focused marketing results.

That said, this should not be where your efforts to effectively advertise your brand on the marketplace end. To establish a significant brand presence on Amazon, you will want to employ brand-awareness marketing through Sponsored Brands ads. This banner ad format is the best out of Amazon's current ad selection for injecting your brand content into the search results landscape.

In our next chapter, we will focus on honing these brand awareness tactics through this ad format to help establish your brand equity on Amazon.

Chapter 11

Build "Top of Funnel" Marketing Momentum with Sponsored Brands

The noblest search of today is the search for excellence.

—Lyndon B. Johnson, 36th U.S. president (1908–1973)

While Sponsored Products are often the bread and butter of an Amazon ad account, if you're looking to increase your brand awareness and are eager to build marketing momentum, don't miss the opportunity to use Sponsored Brands on Amazon. This banner-style ad allows you to express your brand message using logos, customizable ad copy, and featured products. The Sponsored Brands format is available to vendors and those sellers who are enrolled in Amazon's Brand Registry.

Like Sponsored Products, you pay only when a shopper clicks on your ad, but Sponsored Brands ads tend to carry a much higher cost per click (CPC) because of the more prominent placement of these ads on the search results page. Sponsored Brands ads can appear at the top of, alongside, or within the search results. Amazon determines where your ad appears depending on your bid.

When you build a Sponsored Brands campaign, you'll need some sort of baseline for bidding to begin to capture traffic. Amazon will recommend a "suggested bid." While you can certainly adjust up or down from there, I'm generally comfortable getting started with Amazon's suggested bid with two important caveats:

1. You have an airtight daily campaign budget that does not exceed what you're willing to spend. This is critical.
2. You observe your campaign's performance over the next few days and weeks against those "suggested bids" and adjust your bids up or down based on those results (for more help on bid optimization, see Chapter 13).

Think of Sponsored Brands as "top of funnel" marketing, building awareness for your brand and buyer discovery for your products.

Just like with your Sponsored Products campaigns, before you get started, determine how much you want to spend, what products you want to advertise, and what keywords you want to target. Sponsored Brands campaigns are similar to manual Sponsored Products campaigns in that they should be structured around keyword themes.

If you have already created an Amazon Store, you can direct traffic from Sponsored Brands campaigns to your store. This means that when a shopper clicks on a Sponsored Brands ad, they will be taken to your Amazon Store instead of a product list page. You have a couple of options for driving traffic to a store. You can choose to send traffic to the store officially associated with your account, but you can also send customers to a different store. For example, if you have a hybrid account (i.e., if you run ads through first- and third-party accounts), you can use Sponsored Brands in both accounts to drive traffic to your store even though your store lives in only one of those accounts.

CAPTURING NEW CUSTOMERS THROUGH SPONSORED BRANDS

Let's look at how one of my team's clients used a Sponsored Brands campaign to catch the attention of potential customers.

Burke Brands is a high-quality organic coffee company. At their core, they are coffee growers; they have multiple small-batch coffee roasting and packaging facilities while also boasting a state-of-the art cupping lab. Their mission is to "create value for our customers by using the highest-quality green coffee and roasting it to order to ensure maximum freshness."

But as we all know, having a superior product is only a small piece of the marketing puzzle. Because buying on Amazon is becoming second nature to many consumers, they are more likely to start by searching for organic coffee on Amazon before going to a traditional brand's website. The CEO of Burke Brands, Darron Burke, was trying to grow sales and defend the company's position from its competitors. He knew Amazon was only going to become more important in this equation. But with little digital presence and unfamiliarity with Amazon, they reached out to my team for guidance.

"Amazon had become a full-time job, but it was definitely worth it," Burke said. "We could see the return, we could see the sales and the building of brand equity, but we were learning as we went, and it was not extremely organized."

DOS AND DON'TS FOR SPONSORED BRANDS AD COPY SUBMISSIONS

Do

- Use engaging and persuasive ad copy to increase brand awareness and/or educate shoppers on your brand and products.

- Include a call to action when appropriate (e.g., "Shop now").

- Reference the product you are advertising. For example, if you are selling jewelry, you should say, "Treat yourself to luxury jewelry" instead of something vague like "Treat yourself to luxury."

- Capitalize your brand name (you can try submitting ad copy with all the words capitalized if you prefer how that looks, but Amazon usually rejects submissions with unnecessary capitalizations).

- Use the trademark symbol for any terms, logos, etc. that are registered under trademark laws.

Don't

- Make unsupported claims such as "Best Seller" or "#1"—all claims made must appear on the product detail page.

- Reference your competitors.

- Make time-based claims.

- Include a call out to the price or percent discount.

- Use all capital letters or forget to capitalize the first letter of the ad copy.

- Include text errors or misspellings.

They had found the limits of what they knew how to do, but they thought they could gain better traction through a targeted campaign. Our team helped them realize that Sponsored Brands was the way to do it. They were just missing the step of targeting category terms through their ads.

By implementing this strategy, Burke Brands reached a previously untapped gold mine of new potential customers who knew what they wanted but didn't yet know who to buy it from.

Since implementing Sponsored Brands in April 2018, Burke Brands has had five of their best months ever on Amazon. Their flagship offerings, Cafe Don Pablo and Subtle Earth Organic Coffee, have begun to establish themselves as prominent coffee brands. "Overall sales have been growing basically nonstop, every day, every week, and every year," said Burke.

So implementing a Sponsored Brands campaign is something you should absolutely consider when mapping out your advertising strategy. Next, you'll want to closely monitor the campaign's performance.

CLOSELY MONITOR NEWLY LAUNCHED CAMPAIGNS

If Sponsored Brands ads are a new format for your brand, you'll want to closely monitor your results in the days and weeks after launch.

One of my team members had a great analogy for why it's so important to keep a close eye on campaigns that have just launched, especially if it is a new ad format for a brand:

I visualize starting a fire in the woods by hand when I'm launching new ad campaigns. The preparation phase—gathering dry materials (keyword data) and then creating an open space for building the fire (campaign creation) are so important for the longevity of the 'fire.' Then, once a spark is created and the kindling begins to catch (traffic flow), it's so important to ensure you pay close attention to the growing fire—remembering to blow on it and add more material to let it grow (bids and budget increases).

SPONSORED BRANDS CAMPAIGNS FOR SELLERS

To launch a Sponsored Brands campaign in Seller Central, go to the "Advertising" link at the top of the page and then click on "Campaign Manager." Follow the 15 steps below to launch your Sponsored Brands campaign:

1. Click on "Create Campaign."
2. Choose "Sponsored Brands" as the campaign type, as shown in Figure 11–1 on page 101.

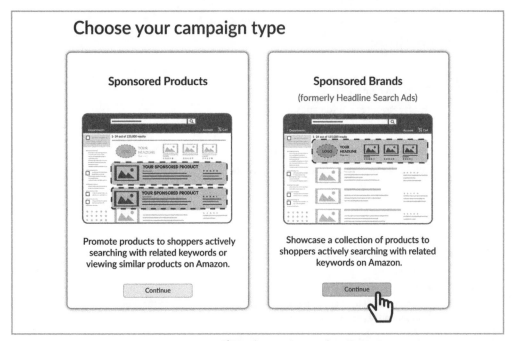

FIGURE 11–1. Choosing a Campaign Type

3. Give your campaign a name that clearly expresses the keyword theme and traffic type.

4. Choose the duration of the campaign, as shown in Figure 11–2 on page 102. We recommend selecting "No End Date" unless there is a specific reason the campaign should end at a certain time.

5. Fill in the daily budget you are willing to spend on this campaign. You can adjust this after the campaign has been launched if needed.

6. Choose the brand for which you are creating this campaign. If you have more than one brand registered in your account, there will be a drop-down list of brands to choose from. You cannot advertise multiple brands within the same Sponsored Brands campaign.

7. You can choose to send traffic to an Amazon Store (including subpages within the store) or a product list page. If you are sending traffic to an Amazon Store, you will need to choose the store and page. If you are sending traffic to a product list page, you will need to search for and add the products you would like to include on that page. You can search by product name or ASIN.

8. Next create your ad copy. Think of how you can best position your brand to the customers you are targeting. For example, if you are targeting category keywords in this campaign, you might want to focus on how you can educate them. I

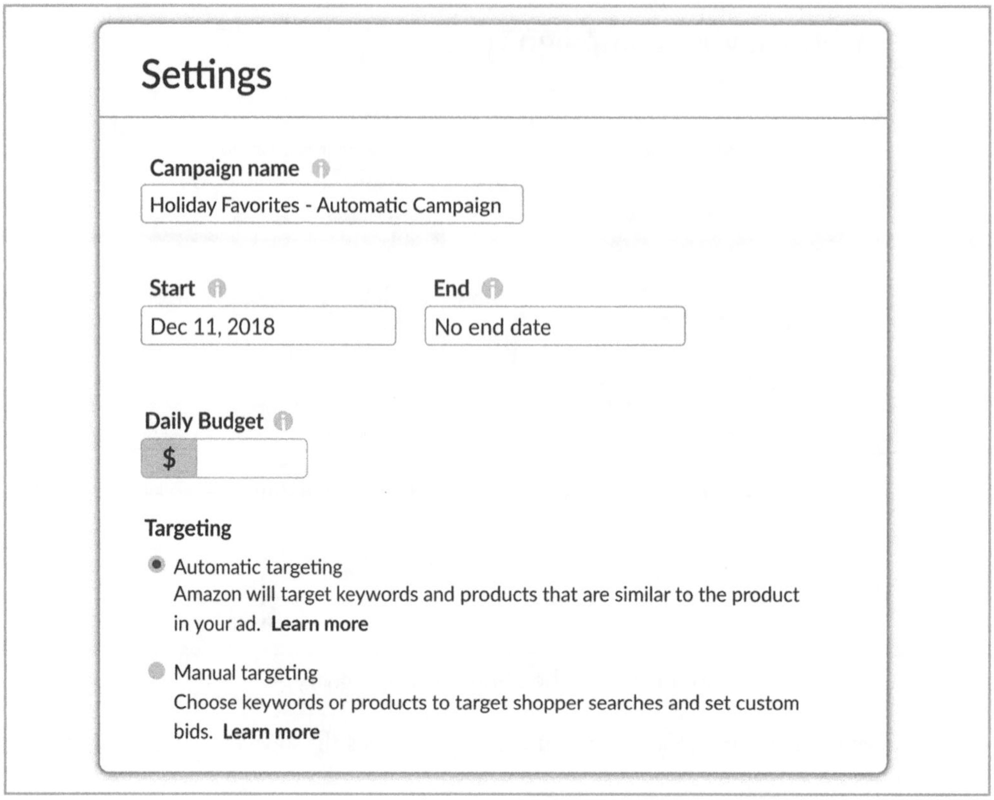

Settings

Campaign name ⓘ

Holiday Favorites - Automatic Campaign

Start ⓘ

Dec 11, 2018

End ⓘ

No end date

Daily Budget ⓘ

$

Targeting

◉ Automatic targeting
Amazon will target keywords and products that are similar to the product in your ad. **Learn more**

◯ Manual targeting
Choose keywords or products to target shopper searches and set custom bids. **Learn more**

FIGURE 11–2. Sponsored Brands Campaign Setup

also suggest using actionable ad copy (e.g., "Shop the latest trends in women's shoes"). Amazon can be strict about any claims you make in the ad copy, as well as your grammar and capitalization, so be careful to adhere to their policies when creating ad copy (https://advertising.amazon.com/resources/ad-policy/en/creative-acceptance).

9. Select and upload the brand logo you would like to use for this ad.

10. Choose the three products you want to feature in the ad, as shown in Figure 11–3 on page 103.

11. You can see a draft of what your ad will look like with the ad copy, brand logo, and featured products. You can also see what it looks like on the desktop, mobile, and app versions. You can also click on the "Other Placements" link to see where else your Sponsored Brands campaign can appear and what it looks like in each placement.

12. Next choose your bids and keywords. Begin by setting a default keyword bid. This bid will apply to keywords as you add them, but you can change the bids for specific keywords after adding the keywords. See Figure 11–4 on page 103.

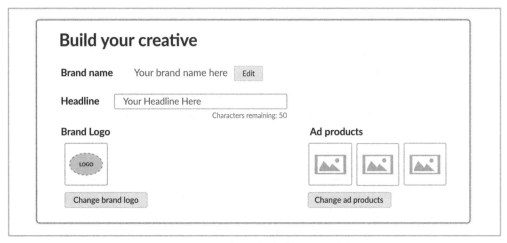

FIGURE 11–3. Choosing Three Products

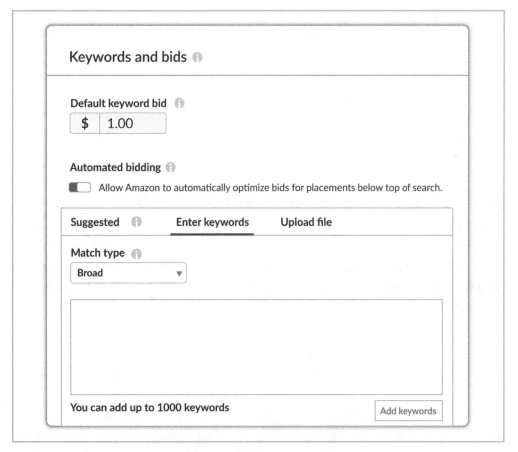

FIGURE 11–4. Keywords and Bids

13. Decide if you would like to enable Automated Bidding. Automated Bidding allows Amazon to lower your bids to improve conversion rates for placements that are below top of search. Amazon will not increase your bids above the limit you set when Automated Bidding is enabled. If you choose not to enable this feature, you can either set a custom bid adjustment or leave the campaign without any bid adjustments. If you want to set a custom bid adjustment, you can choose to increase or decrease bids by a specified amount for placements that are below top of search. For example, a 20-percent decrease on a $5 bid would give you a new bid of $4.

14. Add keywords using either the suggested keywords or by entering a list of keywords. If you are just beginning on Amazon, you might want to consider some of the suggested keywords. Otherwise, we recommend using data from your keyword research to choose which keywords to target.

15. Now review your ad, product list page (if you are using one), and keywords. Once you are satisfied with your Sponsored Brands campaign, click on "Submit for Review" to submit your campaign to Amazon. Amazon will either approve or reject your campaign within 48 hours. If your campaign is approved, it will automatically go live. If your campaign is rejected for any reason, it will be sent to Drafts, where you can make the necessary changes and resubmit it. Amazon does not provide details around why the campaign was rejected, so be sure to double check your campaign settings with Amazon's ad policies (https://advertising.amazon.com/resources/ad-policy/en/creative-acceptance) before re-submitting your campaign.

SPONSORED BRANDS CAMPAIGNS FOR VENDORS

To launch a Sponsored Brands campaign through Vendor Central, go to the "Advertising" link at the top of the page and then click on "Campaign Manager." Follow the 13 steps outlined below to get your campaign up and running. (You may follow Figures 11–1 to 11–3 for guidance with these steps as the primary screens will look the same. Only your choices will be different.)

1. Click on "Create Campaign."
2. Choose "Sponsored Brands" as the campaign type.
3. Give your campaign a name that clearly expresses the keyword theme and traffic type.
4. Choose the duration for the campaign. We recommend running the campaign continuously unless there is a specific reason it should end at a certain time.

5. Set a budget for your campaign. You can set a daily budget or a budget for the entire campaign. If you plan to run this campaign without an end date, you should set a daily budget. Even if you set an end date, we recommend setting a daily budget to allow for greater control over spend. You can adjust the budget after you launch the campaign if needed. You might want to consider setting a budget for the entire campaign if you know that you only have a certain amount of budget to allocate toward this campaign regardless of how long the campaign will run. One major drawback with this setting is that once your campaign has spent the entire budget, the campaign will end and will not run again.

6. Decide on your landing page. You can direct shoppers to a list of products you create, your Amazon Store, or a custom URL on Amazon:
   - *Create a list of products*: Choose at least three products for the landing page. Try to add as many relevant products to this list as you can. A good rule of thumb is to add enough products that a shopper would have a full page or two to browse through. You can preview the landing page once you have added at least three products.
   - *Amazon Store*: If you choose to send traffic from your Sponsored Brands campaign to an Amazon Store, you do not need to choose any products to include at this time.
   - *Custom URL*: You can add a custom URL on Amazon for your landing page. This can be any Amazon page that includes at least three of your products. An example of this might be a custom page that Amazon has created for an upcoming promotion that includes at least 3 of your products.

7. Next create your ad copy. Think of how you can best position your brand to the customers you are targeting. For example, if you are targeting category keywords in this campaign, you might want to focus on how you can educate them. I also suggest using actionable ad copy (e.g., "Shop the latest trends in women's shoes"). Amazon can be strict about any claims you make in the ad copy, as well as your grammar and capitalization, so be careful to adhere to their policies (https://advertising.amazon.com/resources/ad-policy/en/creative-acceptance).

8. Choose a featured image for the ad. This can either be a brand logo or a product image.

9. Select three product images to be shown in the ad. You can change the order of the products by clicking on "Adjust Images" within the preview section.

10. Next choose your bids and keywords. Begin by setting a default keyword bid. This bid will apply to any keywords you add, but you can change it as you are adding keywords.

11. Decide if you would like to enable Automated Bidding. Automated Bidding allows Amazon to lower your bids to improve conversion rates for placements that are below top of search. Amazon will not increase your bids above the bid limit you set when Automated Bidding is enabled. If you choose not to enable this feature, you can either set a custom bid adjustment or leave the campaign without any bid adjustments. If you set a custom bid adjustment, you can choose to increase or decrease bids by a specified amount for placements below top of search. For example, a 20-percent decrease on a $5 bid would give you a new bid of $4.

12. Add keywords by using the suggested keywords, by uploading a file, or by entering a list of keywords manually. If you are just beginning on Amazon, you might want to consider some of the suggested keywords. Otherwise, we recommend using data from your keyword research to choose which keywords to target.

13. After you have reviewed the preview and made any necessary adjustments, you are ready to launch your Sponsored Brands campaign by pressing "Submit for Review." Amazon will either approve or reject your campaign within 48 hours. If your campaign is approved, it will automatically go live. If it is rejected for any reason, it will be sent to Drafts, where you can make the necessary changes and resubmit your campaign.

SPONSORED BRANDS CAMPAIGN: STEP-BY-STEP EXAMPLE

Now that you know how to build a Sponsored Brands campaign for both vendors and sellers, let's walk through a step-by-step example to make it clear.

Regardless of whether you are advertising through Seller Central or Vendor Central, the strategy and structure of your Sponsored Brands campaign will be the same. The main difference between Sponsored Brands campaigns on Seller Central vs. Vendor Central is the technical process of launching the campaign in Amazon's interface. But the steps you take to construct your campaign up to that point are the same.

Let's say you work for Orbit, the popular chewing gum company, and you are interested in launching a Sponsored Brands campaign targeting category traffic to capture new customers who may not be aware of your brand's product offering. The first step will be to decide on the keyword theme for the campaign. In this example, our strategy is to go after high-volume keywords that people might search for when looking for chewing gum, so let's just say our keyword theme is "chewing gum."

Now we will aggregate all category keywords that relate to chewing gum. Some of the keywords included in this theme might be chewing gum, chewing gum bulk, sugar free chewing gum, spearmint chewing gum, etc. If you have already done a Sponsored

Products manual campaign for this same keyword theme, you can use the keywords from that campaign as a starting point for your new Sponsored Brands campaign. Ideally, you want full coverage on all known keywords in Sponsored Products as well as Sponsored Brands.

Given that we are aiming to increase our reach with this Sponsored Brands campaign, we will want to set traditionally tiered bids for all three keyword match types (broad, phrase, and exact). If your approach was extremely targeted, you might want to bid low on broad match keywords or even exclude them entirely. For this example, we will add all keywords in each of the match types with ten-cent increments between broad, phrase, and exact.

If you have the option to send traffic to your Amazon Store, you can choose either a product list page or your store as the landing page. Again, if you were taking an extremely targeted approach, a product list page might be the best option. But in our example, it might make more sense to set the Amazon Store as the landing page so shoppers can be introduced to the Orbit brand through a visually appealing store featuring a variety of related products.

You will need to choose three products for the Sponsored Brands campaign. Since our campaign is being sent to the Amazon Store, you will only need to select products for the ad itself and not for a product list page. I recommend choosing a variety that relate back to the keyword theme to increase the likelihood of showing a shopper what they are looking for. Since the keyword theme of chewing gum is so broad, we might want to include mint chewing gum, bubblegum chewing gum, and even breath mints.

The final step for creating your Sponsored Brands campaign is the ad copy. The copy should refer to the keyword theme, either directly or indirectly, so shoppers can sense the relevancy. Given that our goal for the campaign is to increase brand awareness

HOW TO INCREASE REVENUE OR RANKING FOR SPECIFIC PRODUCTS

If you're looking for an increase in revenue or organic ranking for specific products you sell, and, by virtue of being the brand owner and/or vendor to Amazon, you qualify to use more than just Sponsored Products, you'll want to ensure your products and messaging in each of the (up to) three ad formats align. This means that chosen products are consistent between all ad formats (i.e., you're advertising the same products in Sponsored Products, Sponsored Brands, and Product Display ads).

and acquire new customers, we might want to use the ad copy to educate shoppers on what the brand is or the value it provides. You will want to use the copy to persuade people who are shopping by product type (rather than by brand) that Orbit is the brand for them.

Sponsored Brands Campaign Strategy Options

Take a look at Table 11–1 to see common practices for the two most frequent strategies we employ for Sponsored Brands campaigns within the context of the chewing gum example:

Strategy	Keywords	Landing Page	Ad Copy
Brand Awareness	High-volume keywords (i.e., category keywords such as "chewing gum" or "gum")	Amazon Store or product list page with variety of relevant products	Educate the shopper on your brand and products
Grow Sales at Profitable ACoS	Keywords proved to drive sales at low ACoS (i.e., brand keywords such as "Orbit gum" or "Orbit sugar free gum")	Sub-page of Amazon Store specific to keywords or product list page with only the most relevant products	Persuade the shopper to buy your product

TABLE 11–1. Sponsored Brands Campaign Strategy Options

Now that we have covered how to build out and successfully target traffic segments with Sponsored Brands for both sellers and vendors, let's move on to an even more targeted ad format that is exclusive to brands in a vendor relationship with Amazon: Product Display ads. If you are not a vendor and do not have access to Vendor Central, you can skip to the end of the next chapter for my summary of this section on structure.

Chapter 12

For Vendors Only: Product Display Ads

*The competitor to be feared is one who never bothers about
you at all but goes on making his own business
better all the time.*

—HENRY FORD, FOUNDER OF FORD MOTOR COMPANY (1863–1947)

Do you have a competitor in the marketplace that you wish you
could target directly? Or are you interested in targeting shoppers
with specific interests or in related categories? If you answered yes
to either of these questions, Product Display ads might be the answer you
are looking for.

Available only to vendors, Amazon's Product Display ads can help
attract shoppers and encourage them to take action. These ads appear on
product detail pages, often near the "Add to Cart" button, and display to
shoppers browsing similar products or even existing listings from your
brand.

Whereas Sponsored Products and Sponsored Brands target keywords,
Product Display campaigns target products or interest areas. You can
select specific products on Amazon to reach a narrow group of shoppers,
or you can reach shoppers more broadly through interest-based targeting.

In this chapter, I'll walk you through the basics of what you need to know to make Product Display ads work for your brand.

LEVERAGING BENEFITS WITH PRODUCT DISPLAY ADS

Here are a few ways you can grow your business using Product Display ads:

- *To defend your own product pages.* Target your own product pages by bidding for display placements. If you win the bid for your own page, then you've blocked a competitor from advertising there.
- *As an offensive strategy.* Generate sales for your brand's products by bidding for placement on your *competitors'* product detail pages. Strategically think about how you can position your products against your competitors and use the customizable ad copy in Product Display ads to persuade shoppers to buy your product instead. Consider how your product compares to your competitors' in terms of ratings, reviews, price, product offering, etc. Just like with competitor-targeted campaigns in Sponsored Products or Sponsored Brands, these campaigns will be more expensive and usually run at a higher ACoS. Despite the less profitable nature of these campaigns, there is significant value for your brand when you steal a sale from a competitor and gain a new customer.
- *As a branding play.* Increase your reach on Amazon by going after broader interests or categories to target placements on product pages or elsewhere on the Amazon site. By going after broader categories, you can target shoppers who may have never heard of your brand before.
- *To advertise an upsell or add-on.* Back in the 1970s, McDonald's figured out they could increase their French fry sales by simply asking customers, "Would you like fries with that?" One of the best ways to use Product Display ads is to advertise an upsell to a more expensive and feature-rich version of the product a customer is viewing, or to show them an add-on product that complements their intended purchase.

If you sell to Amazon, Product Display ads are a great format to leverage for all these reasons. But first you have to actually launch the campaign.

HOW TO LAUNCH A PRODUCT DISPLAY AD CAMPAIGN

As a vendor, you can get started by logging in to the Amazon Advertising portal. Then go to the "Advertising" link at the top of the page and click on "Campaign Manager." Follow the ten steps outlined below to launch your Product Display campaign:

1. Click on "Create Campaign," and choose "Product Display Ads" as the campaign ad type, as shown in Figure 12–1 below.

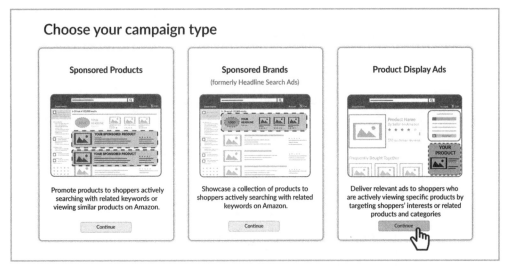

FIGURE 12–1. Choosing a Campaign Type

2. Now decide whether you want to target the campaign by product or interest area.

3. Either way, you'll next select a product to advertise. Search for the product by name, UPC, ASIN, or keyword. You can only choose one product to advertise per campaign.

4. Next choose areas to target (either specific products/product categories or interest areas). See Figure 12–2 on page 112.

   - If you are targeting products on Amazon, you can either target specific products or broader product categories. If you are targeting individual products, you can search for and add them to a customized list of targeted products. If you are targeting related product categories, Amazon will provide a list of categories for you to choose from.

   - If you are targeting interest areas, Amazon will provide a list of shopper interest categories to choose from. You can select just one or many interest areas, depending on how broad you want your campaign's reach to be. See Figure 12–3 on page 112.

5. Give your campaign a name that clearly expresses the product being advertised as well as the targeted product or interest area. We also suggest incorporating the strategy into the campaign name (e.g., 12 Pack Beverage—Competitor ASINs).

6. Set the per-click bid you are willing to pay.

7. Set a budget for your campaign. You can set a daily budget or a budget for the entire campaign. If you plan to run this campaign without an end date, you

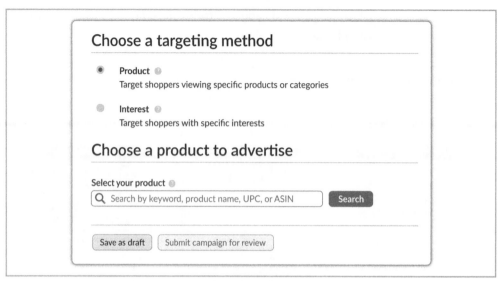

FIGURE 12-2. Choosing a Targeting Method

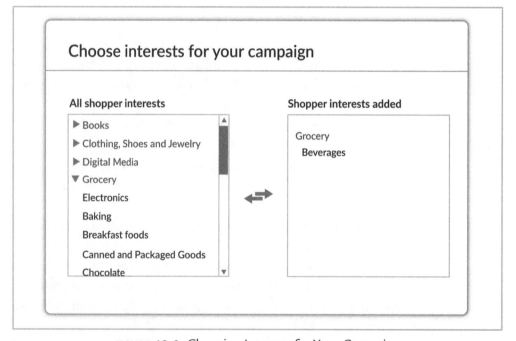

FIGURE 12-3. Choosing Interests for Your Campaign

should set a daily budget. Even if you set an end date, we recommend setting a daily budget to allow for greater control over spend. You can always adjust the budget after you launch the campaign. If you know that you only have a certain amount of budget to allocate toward this campaign (regardless of how long the campaign will run), you might want to consider setting a budget for the entire campaign. One major drawback with this setting is that once your campaign has spent the entire budget, the campaign will end and will not run again.

8. Choose how long you would like the campaign to run. We recommend running the campaign continuously unless there is a specific reason it should end at a certain time.

9. Create and add the headline you will be using for the ad copy.

10. After you have reviewed the preview and made any necessary adjustments, you are ready to launch your Product Display campaign by pressing "Submit Campaign for Review." Just like with Sponsored Brands ads, Amazon will either approve or reject your campaign within 48 hours. If your campaign is approved, it will automatically go live. If it is rejected for any reason, it will be sent to Drafts, where you can then make the necessary changes and resubmit it.

BUILDING YOUR ACCOUNT STRUCTURE

An organized, scalable advertising account structure can help eliminate many of the process headaches associated with Amazon Advertising. As mentioned at the beginning of this section, building out your ad presence within a deliberate campaign structure allows you to think strategically throughout the entire process. From your choice of keywords to traffic segmentation to ad groups to your product mixes and finally to the ad formats at your disposal—the infrastructure of your advertising efforts has been built with your business goals in mind.

But building a robust ad structure is only one part of the process for succeeding on Amazon. The next, equally important step is to effectively optimize within your structure. Taking the necessary actions to nimbly adjust to the competitive landscape, reallocate your budget toward new opportunities within the campaigns, and scale your account for seasonality is paramount for continued success and profitability within this ever-evolving digital space.

Next, we will take an in-depth look at the principles and best practices of optimization.

Chapter 13

Aggregate, Analyze, and Optimize

Never stop testing, and your advertising will never

stop improving.

—DAVID OGILVY, FOUNDER OF LEGENDARY ADVERTISING FIRM

OGILVY & MATHER (1911–1999)

Amazon collects and stores an enormous amount of data analyzing consumer shopping behavior on their site. Some of this data, including reports on search terms, targeting, and advertised products, is available to brands that sell and advertise on Amazon. The insights gained through this data can be leveraged to optimize your advertising efforts.

In this chapter, you'll learn what performance data is available from Amazon, specific optimizations you can make for Sponsored Products and Sponsored Brands ads, and more broadly, how to get more performance out of a fixed budget.

One thing you learn very quickly about companies like Amazon, Google, Facebook, and Microsoft (all of which my company has a formal business relationship with) is their data-driven approach to almost every decision from the food served in their cafeterias to the placement and type of ads on their pages.

My own obsession with data analytics began in fall 1998 in a college physics class when I was working on an Excel project in the library's computer lab. That was the moment I first learned about Google from my physics professor. Before that, I had used a variety of search engines, including Yahoo!, AltaVista, and Excite. Of course, once I started using Google, I found myself using the others far less.

Fast-forward to February 2002, when Google launched their pay-per-click business model for AdWords. I wrote my first ads for a personal project that April. Two months after that, a friend asked me to build a website for him and run Google AdWords ad traffic. That's when I started my digital marketing company.

Back then, my very small company measured everything for clients with a software-based log analyzer tool called Webtrends, which took *hours* to parse through website log files and generate useful reports. By early 2004, my first web programmer discovered another log analyzer tool called Urchin and, after testing it, enthusiastically proclaimed it to be "bloody fast." Not only was it fast, the user interface was intuitive and the reports were easy to interpret, making it ideal for sharing web metrics data with our clients.

In 2005, Google bought Urchin Software Company, rebranded it as Google Analytics, and made it free to use, launching an analytics-based web revolution the world had never seen before.

This data-first revolution has been transformative for business, especially for those firms with access to a robust set of data and a solid analysis and reporting framework. Right now, Amazon's performance data and reporting levels vary, so in some cases, you'll have to do some additional work to fine-tune your campaigns. Let's dig into how that works.

AGGREGATE AMAZON PERFORMANCE DATA

To begin making optimizations in your Amazon Advertising account, you must first pull together the data you'll need. The data in the Amazon interface is fragmented, so you'll need to grab data from multiple reporting menus and compile it in a meaningful way before you can analyze it.

Most reports available on Amazon tie back to Sponsored Products ads because they are Amazon's oldest and most established ad format. In addition, because Sponsored Products ads take shoppers to a single product detail page, reporting on product performance is much easier.

There are fewer data insights available through reports for Sponsored Brands and Product Display ads. In the case of Sponsored Brands, these ads still have relevant reporting on keyword performance and ad placement analysis, but they do not include any reports that touch on the performance of individual products since these ads can direct consumers to a product list page or Amazon Store page containing multiple products to convert on.

Finally, Product Display ads can also target multiple products, so Amazon does not release any granular reporting on which product eventually drove a conversion. As time passes, it is likely that more reports will be released for each of these ad formats.

With this said, you can carry over some of the insights you find in Sponsored Products data to your Sponsored Brands campaigns. For example, there is currently no search query data available for Sponsored Brands, so new keyword opportunities from Sponsored Products can be helpful starting places. Although you can test out new keywords in Sponsored Brands campaigns based on data from Sponsored Products, it is important to keep in mind that keywords and products will not always perform the same across ad types. We will dig deeper into keyword optimization in Chapter 14, but for now, let's look at how to find the most helpful reports for Sponsored Products and Sponsored Brands ads.

All the reports you will need can be accessed either through Seller Central (for sellers) or Vendor Central (for vendors). Look at a combination of advertising reports (e.g., search term reports, targeting reports, advertised product reports, etc.) and account-level reports (e.g., business reports).

Seller Central Performance Data

In Seller Central, you can find the advertising and business reports under the "Reports" link, as shown in Figure 13–1 below.

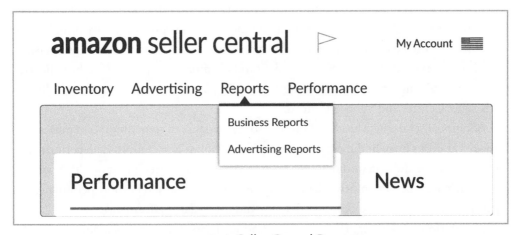

FIGURE 13–1. Seller Central Reports

Vendor Central Performance Data

Vendors can find advertising reports by clicking on the "Advertising" link at the top of the page. Often in Vendor Central you have to request business reports from your Amazon representative. If you are a vendor and don't have access to a business report, you can analyze performance data and make optimizations based on advertising performance reports alone. Most optimizations will come from the advertising reports, but if you do have access to account-level reports, I recommend using this data as well to see the full impact of advertising.

Attribution Sales Against Ad Clicks

An *attribution model* is a rule, or set of rules that determine how credit for conversions (i.e., sales) is assigned to touch points along the conversion path. Amazon uses something called *last touch attribution* to track a shopper's activity after they click on an ad in case they purchase the product later. In last touch attribution, credit is given to the final touch point (or click) that immediately preceded the sale. That is how sales can be attributed to a click even if the purchase occurred days after the initial click. Attribution in Seller Central and Vendor Central varies, so it is also important to keep the attribution window in mind when making optimizations.

In Seller Central, the standard attribution window is seven days for Sponsored Products and 14 days for Sponsored Brands, while in Vendor Central, the attribution window is 14 days for Sponsored Products, Sponsored Brands, and Product Display campaigns.

Attribution Example for a Sponsored Brands Campaign

Let's look at an example of attribution for a Sponsored Brands campaign. Let's say that your brand sells high-end kitchen appliances. Because your products have a high price point, it's not unusual for shoppers to do some research on Amazon before purchasing. If a shopper clicked on your Sponsored Brands campaign on August 1 but did not purchase until August 8, this would be captured by the 14-day attribution window in both Seller Central and Vendor Central.

Additionally, sales data has a 48-hour lag, so recent data can sometimes seem misleading if looked at on its own. In the example above, if you looked at month-to-date performance data on August 4, the data would not represent actual performance since it would show four days' worth of spend but only two days of sales. In this case, it would be more helpful to look at the past week's performance rather than the month-to-date performance.

At the time of writing, there are no Product Display reports available under the "Advertising Reports" link in Vendor Central. However, you can download a report of daily campaign performance metrics from the "Reports" link after clicking on an individual Product Display campaign.

If you have a connection to Amazon's application programming interface (API), a system of resources that allows developers to create data connections for building software, the data you see through the API might vary from what you see in the interface or in Amazon's reports. This API connection could be through a tool that helps manage your Amazon Advertising account, or it could be through an agency or similar resource. Just remember that the numbers you see in each of these may not always match exactly, and that is to be expected.

ANALYZING THE DATA

Once you have aggregated all the reports you need, you can begin analyzing the data. You can glean valuable insights from sales, traffic, and search term data and then use those to optimize your account. By analyzing these reports, you can identify opportunities to:

- Increase or decrease keyword bids to improve profitability or grow sales
- Expand keyword coverage based on search queries
- Add or exclude products to show the strongest products on the most relevant search terms
- Implement negative keywords to reduce unprofitable spend

Keep in mind as you make optimizations from these reports that keywords and products must receive at least one click in order to appear in the data. This is important because it is possible that keywords or products that are not included in the reports also need to be optimized. For example, if a broad match keyword is currently bid too low to receive traffic, it will not appear in the reports, but if the bid were raised, it could potentially give you a very profitable return.

Using Bulk Operations

Amazon allows you to make bulk changes to your account by using bulk operations. Once you understand the process, it can save you time in your routine optimizations.

To get started with bulk operations in Seller Central, navigate to the "Campaign Manager" link and then click on "Bulk Operations," shown in Figure 13–2 on page 120.

You can then either download a bulk file of the account or a bulk template. A bulk file of the account will consist of a spreadsheet with all the campaign data. Because most bulk uploads consist of new keyword, ad group, and campaign creations, we have usually just downloaded the template and created a bulk file from scratch. But if you are seeking to make large-scale changes to existing campaigns (e.g., changing

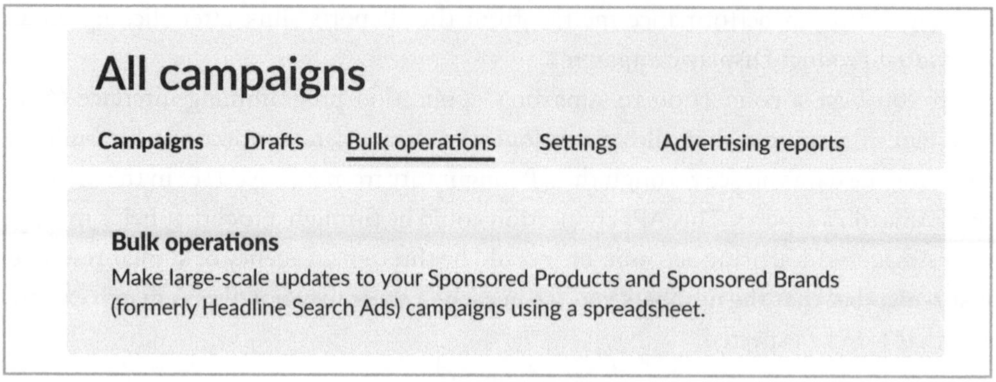

FIGURE 13-2. Bulk Operations

bids or the status of ads), you might want to download a bulk file so you have all the campaign data you need.

If you download a bulk file of the account, you can make changes to the file and then upload the revised version. When downloading the file in Seller Central, choose a time frame within the past 60 days.

Once you have downloaded the file, you can begin drafting the bulk upload. The data you will need to include depends on whether you are creating a new campaign, ad group, keyword, or ad/product. Here's what you will need to include for each:

- *Campaigns*: campaign name, daily budget, start date (MM/DD/YYYY), end date (this can be left blank if the campaign will run continuously), targeting type (auto or manual), campaign status (enabled, paused, or archived), and bidding strategy (on or off)
- *Ad Groups*: campaign name, ad group name, max bid (default bid), and ad group status (enabled, paused, or archived)
- *Keywords*: campaign name, ad group name, max bid, keyword, match type (broad, phrase, exact, negative phrase, or negative exact), and status (enabled, paused, or archived)
- *Ads/Products*: campaign name, ad group name, SKU, and status (enabled, paused, or archived)

If you are not making any changes at the campaign level, you can leave this row of data out completely. For example, if you are adding more keywords to an existing campaign, you only need to include the data at the ad group, keyword, and ad level. The same rule goes for adding new products or keywords—you only need to include the rows that have new data.

Bulk operations are also available to vendors. The bulk upload feature is especially helpful for making large-scale updates and changes to your Vendor Central account.

Navigate to the "Advertising" link in Vendor Central and then click on "Bulk Operations." Just as in Seller Central, you can download a bulk file of the account or a template to start from scratch.

If you have never used bulk operations before, you will need to activate this feature in your account before you can begin. You can activate bulk operations by clicking on "Advertising," then "Bulk Operations," and then click on "Activate My Account." Amazon will process your request and notify you when it is available.

When downloading a bulk file of your account, you will need to select a time frame within the past 60 days. You can exclude terminated campaigns or campaigns with zero impressions from the download. We recommend excluding terminated campaigns (since you probably don't need to make changes to campaigns that are no longer running), but we generally find it helpful to include data from campaigns that have zero impressions so you can continue to optimize this data.

Once you download a bulk file, you can review the file, make any necessary changes in Excel, and then save it on your local drive. Any campaigns you do not make changes to will continue to operate as they did before. To upload a revised file, go back to the "Bulk Operations" section in Vendor Central and click on the button to choose a file from your local drive. Once you have selected the file, you can upload it to be processed.

Whether in Vendor Central or Seller Central, bulk operations can save you lots of time in building out and optimizing your account.

OPTIMIZATIONS FOR SPONSORED PRODUCTS

Now that you've been briefly introduced to the types of reports available in Amazon's interface, let's go over the various optimizations you can make with the data insights from these reports. We'll start with optimizations for Sponsored Products.

Here are the top six reports you'll want to run:

1. *The Sponsored Products Search Term Report* can give you insights into what customers on Amazon are searching for when looking for your products. This report can be used to mine new keyword opportunities based on high-converting customer search terms.
2. *The Sponsored Products Advertised Product Report* can help you see the amount of traffic and sales coming through your brand by ASIN. This is a great resource for analyzing the amount and profitability of traffic flowing to a specific listing.
3. *The Sponsored Products Targeting Report* can be used to gauge how often keywords are being triggered by searches and how the search volume has changed over time. This report can shine a light on any adjustments you should make to keyword bids based on the traffic levels flowing through your keywords.

4. *The Sponsored Products Purchased Product Report* can reveal new advertising and targeting opportunities by showing what ASINs shoppers are converting on after clicking on one of your products' ads. This helps find relevant products that may work well in a bundle due to a history of clicks from one ASIN to the other. This report is currently only available in Seller Central.

5. *The Sponsored Products Placement Report* shows where your ads are appearing within the search results. This report can be used to ensure you are winning the top ad slot consistently if you are running a campaign with aggressive bids. This is also great for ensuring that a launch campaign is gaining visibility. Although not in the top four reports, this report is still useful as it provides details on campaign performance based on where the Sponsored Products ad was placed (Top of Search—the first ad placements on the top of the first page, Rest of Search—any placement below the fold on page one and subsequent pages, or on a Product Detail Page—any placement on a product's page). Amazon is known for constantly testing new placements behind the scenes often without the seller's knowledge. With this report, you can compare the traffic from the top of search with that of other placements and evaluate the results.

6. *The Business Reports* available in Seller Central allow you to view data for the entire account rather than just the advertising performance. The most useful business report is the Detail Page Sales and Traffic Report by ASIN. You can combine this data with the data in the advertising reports to get a better picture of how your advertising is impacting your overall sales and to identify areas of opportunity to increase or decrease advertising aggression or spend on certain products. We will cover Amazon's business reports in more detail in Chapter 19.

OPTIMIZATIONS FOR SPONSORED BRANDS

The types of optimizations you will make to Sponsored Brands campaigns will be different from the ones you'll make to Sponsored Products ads. For one, since there is no search query data available for Sponsored Brands, you will take a different approach to keyword optimizations. For another, unlike Sponsored Products, you can customize and test aspects of the ad itself (such as ad copy, brand images, product images, etc.).

Keyword Optimizations and Product Alignment

Because search query data is not currently available for Sponsored Brands campaigns, the most helpful report for Sponsored Brands is the Targeting Report.

The Sponsored Brands Targeting Report is similar to the Sponsored Products Targeting Report and can be used the same way to analyze your campaigns. You can gauge the search volume flowing through each keyword, how it has changed over time, and any opportunities to increase or decrease the keyword bid.

For example, if you see in the Sponsored Brands Targeting Report that a keyword has only received a handful of impressions or clicks, you might want to consider how relevant that keyword is to the products that are being advertised. You can also check your bidding strategy by using the Sponsored Brands Keyword and Campaign Placement Reports, which will show you where your campaigns are showing and whether they are winning placements at the top of search or below the fold. Based on this analysis, you might consider increasing the keyword bid to be more competitive and increase your ad's chance of appearing at the top of the search results when that keyword is triggered.

If you see that most of your budget is being spent on just one keyword, you might want to reconsider targeting this keyword within the campaign. Even if you are willing to spend more on the campaign, it is difficult to gauge how much you would need to increase the budget to ensure that your other keywords get traffic. You may decide this keyword is spending more than it is worth and end up pausing it within the campaign.

You don't need high traffic levels to have successful Sponsored Brands campaigns. You just need the proper keyword-product alignment so you can show shoppers who are looking for products like yours exactly what they are searching for.

Ensuring Your Sponsored Brands Visibility

As described above in the step-by-step process for setting up your Sponsored Brands campaigns, automated bidding can help increase your impressions by taking advantage of other Sponsored Brands placements outside of top of search. With this said, if it is your intention to achieve prominent placement at the top of search, you might want to consider turning automated bidding off. My team has experienced lower click-through rates and lower conversion rates when automated bidding is turned on because of the spike in impressions from other placements. In order to have more control over the volume of impressions and spend going toward other placements (outside of top of search), we recommend setting custom bid adjustments for placements below top of search. See Figure 13–3 on page 124.

Adding Keywords to a Sponsored Brands Campaign

One indication that you need to add a search query to your Sponsored Brands campaign is if most of the traffic for a keyword is funneling through the broad or phrase match. In this case, you should cross-reference with the Sponsored Products Search Term Report

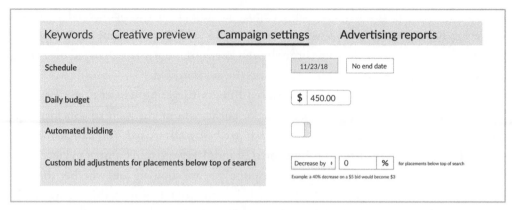

FIGURE 13–3. Setting Custom Bid Adjustments

to identify any high-traffic terms in your Sponsored Products campaign that do not yet have keyword coverage in Sponsored Brands.

Another metric to consider when optimizing your Sponsored Brands campaigns is the clickthrough rate (CTR). The CTR is the percentage of people who saw your ad and then clicked on it. It is calculated by dividing the number of clicks by the number of impressions. If you have a very low CTR, it could be your ad is not as relevant as you first suspected, based on the keywords that are being targeted and the ad that is being shown. If you run into this issue, try doing a test search on Amazon for that keyword, and then compare the results page to your product offering and ad.

If you add keywords to Sponsored Brands campaigns based on search query data from Sponsored Products, it is important to monitor the performance of those keywords using the Sponsored Brands Targeting Report.

Ad Testing and Optimization

Additionally, Sponsored Brands campaigns can be optimized in a way that is not supported within Sponsored Products. The Sponsored Brands ad itself, as well as the landing page, can be adjusted and optimized (by changing the logo, ad copy, and product images) rather than just the keyword optimizations that Sponsored Products ads are limited to.

As part of making optimizations to your Sponsored Brands campaigns, you can try testing different aspects of your ads to see how they perform. Although Amazon does not currently allow true split tests, our hope is that this will one day be an option. In the meantime, you can test the performance of campaigns when certain elements are changed by creating two almost identical campaigns but with one difference (either in the ad copy, landing page, brand image, or product images) and then gauging the success of each. This is usually done when the volume is significant.

We have usually found when running simultaneous tests that one campaign will gain traction and take off while the other does not get a real chance at converting. Because of this, we have tried running tests at separate times to give both campaigns a fair shot. The caveat with this approach is that you need to be sure to avoid any period of high seasonality. For example, if one campaign ran during June and one during July, chances are the second one will outperform the first if your brand experiences a spike for Prime Day, which takes place in mid-July.

Elements to Test in Sponsored Brands Campaigns

Here are four elements you can test in Sponsored Brands campaigns:

1. *Ad copy*. You might want to test out a few different tag lines in the ad copy to see which one performs best.
2. *Main image*. You can test how a brand logo performs vs. a product image. Some Sponsored Brands placements, such as on the mobile app, only show the main image and the ad copy. With this in mind, you might want to test how shoppers convert when they are shown the brand logo vs. an image of the product.
3. *Product images*. Sponsored Brands campaigns allow you to show three product images to the right of the ad copy. You might want to test how showing different products here (or even the same products but in a different order) performs.
4. *Landing page*. You can test the impact of directing shoppers to different landing pages. If you have an Amazon Store, you might want to test how an ad performs when it directs to the store vs. a product list page. You might also want to test how different product list pages perform.

Additionally, when making optimizations to your Sponsored Brands campaigns, you should evaluate how persuasive, engaging, and actionable your ad copy is. If you decide that there is room to improve the ad copy, you will need to launch a new Sponsored Brands campaign.

At this time, you cannot make changes to the ad copy, products, or images in a Sponsored Brands campaign once the campaign has been launched. You must launch a new campaign in order to make these changes. You can, however, make adjustments and additions to keywords and keyword bids in Sponsored Brands campaigns without having to launch a new campaign.

Sponsored Brands campaigns can be great to fully leverage during holidays or periods of peak seasonality, but there should also be a baseline of these campaigns that are always running. You don't want to miss out on opportunities to gain sales through Sponsored Brands on a typical day. Customers shop year-round, so it only makes sense to be visible to shoppers year-round as well. You should consider having brand, category, and competitor campaigns running at all times.

INCREASE PERFORMANCE WITH SMART BIDS

Once you've studied the data, one of the broader themes to increasing the return on your advertising account is to spend more time and money on the winners and less (or no more) money on the losers. It's the foundation of effective performance marketing and likely the core premise of optimizing business performance and growth overall.

What this means in a practical sense is to bid higher for keywords that:

- Already enjoy a lower ACoS than your maximum ACoS target.
- Have a medium to large traffic volume (this gives you statistically significant data as well as a material amount of traffic to move the needle).
- Have room to increase your position (i.e., a higher position so you get more clicks) or your impression share. Keywords that are not currently receiving many impressions or clicks may need an increased bid to compete for ad placements. By increasing the bids for keywords with low levels of traffic, you are also increasing the likelihood that they will appear in related searches and therefore increasing impressions and clicks. If you do not increase your bids for keywords that fall into this bucket, they may never realize their full potential.

Here are some examples to make this clear.

Let's say you sell camping equipment on Amazon, and your ACoS goal is 10 percent. Some of your top keywords for tents might include "tent," "4 person tent," "waterproof tent," etc.

In Table 13–1 on page 127, the keyword "tent" is currently driving sales at a 6 percent ACoS. Since this is below your ACoS goal of 10 percent, there is still room to get more aggressive on this keyword by increasing the keyword bid.

The keyword "2 person tent" has only received 129 impressions and one click. This is an area where you would want to increase your impression share by increasing your bid to ensure that it has a chance to compete for ad placements.

Because Amazon revenue data is on a 48-hour lag, you'll want to optimize your bids at least monthly and perhaps as often as weekly, depending on your ad-driven click volume, to give yourself enough time to analyze the available data. Once you have adjusted your bids, a good rule of thumb is to wait a week before making any other changes for those keywords. It is important to give your most recent changes time to perform so you to see the results before making further adjustments.

Keyword	Impressions	Clicks	Spend	Avg. CPC	Sales	ACoS
tent	7,333	23	$20	0.87	$325	6 percent
camping tent	9,845	47	$35	0.74	$360	10 percent
4 person tent	2,178	11	$8	0.73	$115	7 percent
waterproof tent	1,455	8	$5	0.63	$0	
2 person tent	129	1	$1	1.00	$0	

TABLE 13–1. Keyword Performance Results

PEEL AND STICK FOR AMAZON AD CAMPAIGNS

In addition to bidding more for winning keywords that are not already achieving maximum traffic, you can "break out" those few that are crushing it into their own unique ad group or campaign to generate even more clicks and revenue.

In the *Ultimate Guide to Google AdWords* by Perry Marshall (2017, Entrepreneur Press), the author coined the term "peel-and-stick" to describe this very tactic for those optimizing their Google ad campaigns.

Essentially, with peel-and-stick, you take the few keywords generating most of your traffic, peel them off, and stick each into its own ad group.

Peel-and-stick also ties into the 80–20 rule—also known as the Pareto principle—which says that 80 percent of effects can be attributed to 20 percent of the causes. This peel-and-stick process allows you to find the 20 percent of keywords that drive 80 percent of the traffic and then focus your efforts on those areas of the account.

For Sponsored Products, this means more campaigns and fewer ad groups per campaign. If you are just getting started with advertising on Amazon, you might want to have coverage on many keywords in the same campaign to see which ones gain the most traction and then peel and stick those keywords into their own campaign. If you notice that nearly all spend or revenue is flowing through just a few keywords, it is time to consider launching them in their own campaign, which can be optimized separately to build on its previous success.

Optimizations for these new Sponsored Products campaigns will focus on increasing the granularity of these keywords through keyword-product alignment.

Peel-and-Stick Process Example

Let's say your original campaigns included all your men's shoe products and all keywords relating to men's shoes (men's casual shoes, dress shoes, running shoes, etc.). Let's say that the keyword "men's running shoes" proved to drive most of the traffic in this campaign. See Table 13–2 on page 129 for what this might look like.

With the peel-and-stick process, you would break out the top keyword from the overarching shoes campaign and create a new campaign centered on it. This new campaign would include the keyword that was driving most of the traffic in the old campaign (e.g., men's running shoes) along with keywords that followed the same theme (e.g., running shoes for men). In the new campaign, you would only include products that are running shoes. This would allow you to separate out the areas of the account that are driving most of the traffic and make optimizations that will actually move the needle.

The strategy for peel-and-stick in Sponsored Brands is very similar. The main difference is that once you peel and stick specific keyword themes and products into a new campaign, you can also get more targeted in your approach through the ad copy. To continue with the running shoes example, your original Sponsored Brands campaign for all men's shoes might have had ad copy that was generic to all types of men's shoes, such as "Enjoy every step with [brand name]." In your new campaign, you can use the ad copy to directly speak to customers who are looking for men's running shoes (e.g., "Experience comfort and support while you run").

Now that you've learned how to aggregate, analyze, and optimize, it's time to learn about keyword-level optimizations. And that's the subject of our next chapter.

Keyword	Clicks	Percent of Sales
men's running shoes	3,551	48.8 percent
running shoes for men	2,127	29.6 percent
men's shoes	964	7.7 percent
men's dress shoes	721	5.7 percent
men's sandals	497	4.7 percent
casual men's shoes	109	1.0 percent
loafers for men	95	0.9 percent
dress shoes for men	34	0.3 percent
men's flip flops	28	0.3 percent
golf shoes for men	26	0.2 percent
casual shoes for men	23	0.2 percent
men's golf shoes	19	0.2 percent
sandals for men	17	0.2 percent
brown dress shoes for men	16	0.2 percent
men's loafers	11	0.1 percent

TABLE 13–2. Keyword Performance Data

Chapter 14

Keyword Optimizations

> *There is your audience. There is the language.*
> *There are the words that they use.*
>
> —EUGENE M. SCHWARTZ, ADVERTISING COPYWRITER, AUTHOR (1927–1995)

Although we covered the research and acquisition phase of keywords in Chapter 8, in this chapter we'll be discussing keyword optimizations. Adding the keywords to your account is only the first step in the process. To succeed in your keyword targeting, you will need to optimize your keywords on an ongoing basis.

There are three primary methods for keyword optimization:

1. Keyword bid optimization
2. Adding negative keywords
3. Adding phrase and exact match keyword variations

Let's explore each method in detail.

KEYWORD BID OPTIMIZATION

If you are just getting started on Amazon, you will quickly learn that keyword bids, much like keyword research, require consistent attention.

Even mature accounts that have been running for years require bid adjustments. The competitive landscape is always changing, so you need to always be aware of how much you are paying for each click and how that relates to your ad visibility and your overarching advertising strategies.

You might want to follow a work flow such as the one described below when making bid optimizations:

- First, find areas where you need to lower bids to maintain profitability. Look for keywords that are spending a significant amount but have an ACoS higher than your desired range. You will want to lower the CPC bid for these keywords since they are currently unprofitable.

- Next, look for areas to get more aggressive with bids where keyword profitability is exceptional. Perhaps a keyword is performing well but has low levels of traffic. In this case, it might be able to gain more traffic at a profitable ACoS if you increase your bid.

- Finally, look for areas that have received hardly any traffic. Because these keywords have not received much traffic, it is likely they will not have produced a sale yet, so you will not have an ACoS to reference. You will therefore want to test how they perform when you increase their bid. Ideally, these keywords will begin to gain traction as you increase the bid, and you will then have a better idea of their profitability. Long tail keywords that are extremely specific will typically receive less traffic than more general head term keywords. Keep this in mind as you make optimizations, and be careful not to continually increase the bid for long tail keywords in the hopes of increasing traffic beyond levels they can support.

Just as you examine and optimize keyword bids in your manual campaigns, you will also want to optimize your bids in your automatic campaigns. Since automatic campaigns do not contain keywords, however, you will not manage the bids at the keyword level. Instead, bids are set at the ad group level. You can follow the same work flow described above to make bid optimizations for ad groups in automatic campaigns.

If you are making bid adjustments by hand rather than through an automatic bidding tool, it is highly unlikely you will have the time to comb through every keyword and ad group in your account, and that's OK! The key is to focus on the keywords and ad groups that will make the biggest impact. This goes back to the 80-20 rule we discussed at the end of Chapter 13. Your time is best spent optimizing the handful of keywords that drive most of your traffic.

ADDING NEGATIVE KEYWORDS

When you type a search phrase into a keyword-driven search engine like Amazon (or a traditional search engine like Google), it's often not clear to the engine what you're *really* looking for. Although most modern languages allow for very high levels of precision, many of us use search terms that are far less precise. We do this because many times we really don't know enough yet about the product or idea we're interested in to describe it in the most exact way.

One way to ensure you're getting the most qualified traffic for your products is to add negative keywords. A *negative keyword* is a keyword that prevents your ad from being triggered by a certain word or phrase. Your ads aren't shown to anyone who is searching for that phrase, and thus it acts as a filter for your search traffic.

Adding negative keywords is crucial for eliminating wasteful spend within Sponsored Products. (Unfortunately, as of this writing, you cannot add negative keywords to automatic campaigns in Vendor Central—only to automatic campaigns in Seller Central.)

First, let's define "wasteful spend." I define it as any spend on traffic that is unintentional and irrelevant to your product category or any ongoing strategy within your campaigns. The most explicit example of this type of spend is on unrelated keywords.

Wasteful spend is *not* any spend dedicated to testing out new strategies, a new variation of keyword, or an adjusted product mix. Though these tests may not prove to be fruitful, you still learned valuable lessons about your advertising strategy and how to further adjust to meet your business goals.

Though automatic campaigns are an extremely valuable tool for keyword research and product visibility, Amazon's algorithm can still catch search terms and ad placements that are totally irrelevant to your product category. The same can be said for broad match keywords—there may be significant overlap between terms for a certain broad match keyword and a completely unrelated keyword meant for a separate product category.

Negative Keyword Example

Let's say you're on the marketing team for a large detergent brand, and you have both automatic and manual campaigns set up for your line of detergent pods. After they run for a few days, you download a search term report to analyze the traffic flow by looking at top-spending customer search terms that did not convert. You notice that a significant amount of spend is being allocated for the term "coffee pods" (shown in Table 14–1 on page 134). This unrelated traffic is flowing through both your automatic

Keyword	Customer Search Term	Clicks	Spend	Revenue
N/A (automatic campaign)	Coffee pods	155	$132	$0
Detergent pod - broad match	Coffee pods	38	$37	$0

TABLE 14–1. Finding Negative Keywords to Add

campaign via Amazon's algorithm and your broad match term "detergent pods" within your manual campaign.

This is the perfect time to set up some negative keywords to ensure this wasteful spend will not occur in the future. Simply adding "coffee pods" and its variations as "Negative Exact" keywords will prevent your ad from ever showing for these terms.

Finding Keywords to Add as Negatives

The first step to using negative keywords to filter out this traffic is to mine for these keywords in your search term report. Download a search term report for the past 60 days of campaign activity. Sort the report by how much you spend on each keyword and then filter it to only show terms that your campaigns have spent on with zero conversions. The list of customer search terms and the keywords they flowed through should be much shorter now. If you come across a keyword that is very much related to your product category but has yet to lead to a sale, consider lowering bids if the spend is too high for your budget before adding it as a negative keyword.

You will most likely see a fair number of ASINs within the Customer Search Term column of this narrowed-down field. This may initially appear to be customers searching by ASIN. In reality, it is listing placement traffic driven by your campaigns.

On product listings, there is a "Products Related to this Item" bar as well as a "Sponsored Products Related to this Item." The latter is populated by Sponsored Products traffic that Amazon's algorithm has deemed relevant. Unfortunately, there is currently no method to filter out certain ASIN traffic via negatives, so if you notice an ASIN with high spend that is unrelated to your product category, consider adding the product's brand name or most general category descriptor to your negative keywords.

Once you find an unrelated search term flowing through either a manual keyword match type or an automatic campaign, make a note of the term and the specific campaign and ad group the traffic is flowing through. Return to the Campaign Manager interface, as shown in Figure 14–1 below, and navigate to the campaign and ad group the term is being triggered in. You will want to first add the negative keyword here, but you may want to add it to other campaigns that are advertising similar products as well.

FIGURE 14–1. Returning to Campaign Manager Interface

Once you've arrived at the interface to add negative keywords, you will want to decide which match type of negative keyword to use. Negative keywords can be set up for both phrase match and exact match types. A negative phrase match keyword, much like a normal phrase match keyword, will filter out any search terms that contain the keyword or phrase in the same order even if there are additional words on either side of the phrase. For instance, adding a negative phrase match keyword for "coffee pods" will filter both "coffee pods" and any variations such as "small coffee pods" or "hazelnut coffee pods." A negative phrase match keyword will *not* filter out traffic such as "pods for coffee makers."

Here are the outlined steps for adding negative keywords to an existing campaign:

1. Within the campaign manager, open up a Sponsored Products campaign.
2. For Sellers, once in the campaign, navigate to the Negative Keywords tab.
   - For Vendors, you will navigate to the Negative Targeting tab (see Figure 14–2).

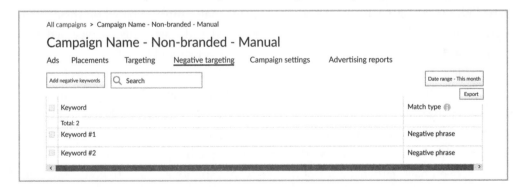

FIGURE 14–2. Navigating to Negative Targeting

3. Once in this tab, you can add either Phrase or Exact match negative keywords.

4. For Sellers, you can also add negative keywords at the ad group level.

ADDING PHRASE AND EXACT MATCH KEYWORD VARIATIONS

One of the biggest challenges in Amazon's current advertising interface is gaining full clarity on where traffic is flowing. It is easy to fall into the mindset that if your campaigns are performing well, you do not need to dig into *how* they are performing well.

Though I certainly do not recommend *over*-optimizing your campaigns (by, say, conducting bid optimizations more than twice a week), the above mindset is a recipe for disaster. Understanding how and where traffic flows through your campaigns, keywords, and match types is not only incredibly important for fixing any issues or problem areas but also for discovering and capitalizing on new opportunities to increase growth or profitability.

With increased clarity comes increased control. When you can easily and routinely identify new keyword opportunities, acting on them and getting the results you desire becomes much simpler.

A great way to exert this control and further optimize your campaigns is by breaking out new keyword variations. Let's say you have created a manual campaign targeting category traffic with broad, phrase, and exact match types for the keyword "mattress protector." After a few weeks, you notice that a large share of impressions and clicks are flowing through the phrase and broad match types but not through the exact match. However, the exact match type is still more profitable than the other two.

Identifying Keywords to Add

To investigate this further, you will need to pull a search term report and identify what unique terms are flowing through these broad and phrase match keywords. This process is similar to searching for negative keywords, but in this scenario we are looking for terms that we believe will perform well in our manual campaign based on their initial performance in the auto campaign or in the broad and phrase match type. Refer to Figure 14–3 on page 137 to see what pulling this report should look like.

Sorting your search term report in Excel by clicks, revenue, or conversions is a great way to identify top-performing terms. Adding a filter for an ACoS range within your business goals will narrow this list down even further. The Campaign Name, Ad Group Name, and Match Type columns will always tell you where a search term's traffic was caught within your campaigns and through which match type.

Once you have gathered a list of new keyword variations to add to your campaign, you need to ensure they are correctly categorized based on traffic type, product mix, and

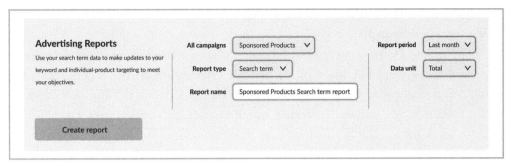

FIGURE 14–3. Pulling the Advertising Report

priority before adding them to your campaign. Repeat this process for any task involving the creation of new keywords, whether through breaking out variations or through keyword research.

Refer back to Chapter 8 to ensure you have all three keyword match types included in your campaigns and are aware of their distinctive qualities.

Keyword optimization is one of the lowest-level optimizations you can make. In the next chapter, we'll take it up a notch and help you understand how to make changes at the account and campaign level that will help you increase your volume and profit.

Adjusting Your Keyword Bidding Strategy

In early 2019, Amazon released a beta tool for enhanced bidding strategies that advertisers can deploy on new Sponsored Products campaigns or adjust for older Sponsored Products campaigns. The strategies allow advertisers to give Amazon's algorithm discretion on adjusting their keyword bids based on the likelihood of driving a conversion.

Advertisers can choose from a "Down Only," "Up and Down," or a "Fixed Bid" strategy. The "Fixed Bid" strategy is the pre-update default setting for bids—meaning if you want your keyword bids to remain untouched by Amazon's algorithm as if this update never occurred, this is the setting you should choose. This means that Amazon will not adjust your bid for the likelihood of a conversion. This may not lead to an increase of conversions, but a decrease in conversion rate since you are not using Amazon's algorithmic adjustments.

The "Down Only" strategy gives Amazon's algorithm permission to only adjust your bids down based on the increased likelihood of driving a conversion. For example, if you are a watch brand and have a $1 bid for the keyword "sports watch," Amazon may decrease your bid if the keyword is capturing traffic from a less relevant customer search term (e.g., "sports watch band") or is bidding for a placement that has not historically performed as well for your products, as well as other conversion factors that Amazon has not made public. This is a conservative strategy that may be suitable for advertisers that have a strict budget and ACoS goal.

The "Up and Down" strategy gives the algorithm the freedom to either decrease or increase your keyword bid based on its predicted likelihood of conversion. Using the watch brand example again, if you have a $1 bid on "sports watch" and that captures traffic from a highly relevant customer search term (e.g., "mens sports watch") or is bidding on a historically high-converting placement, Amazon has the discretion to increase your bid up to $2 for placements at the top of search and up to $1.50 for other placements below the fold and on subsequent pages. You also give Amazon the discretion to lower your bid based on the same model described in the "Down Only" strategy.

These updated strategies can bring increased profitability or visibility to your keyword-driven Sponsored Products campaigns depending on your business and advertising goals. As with any updated feature in the Amazon interface, I recommend testing these strategies out conservatively and expanding their usage incrementally as many of these tools are likely to evolve and change as Amazon continues to improve their data and algorithm.

Chapter 15

Account and Campaign-Level Optimizations

By optimizing for customer success, you're more than likely optimizing for growth. And if your revenue doesn't grow along with your customer success metrics, then you're probably doing something wrong.

—ALEX TURNBULL, FOUNDER OF GROOVE SOFTWARE COMPANY (1982–)

Most of the optimizations we have discussed so far have been related to keyword changes and bid changes at either the keyword or ad group level. Although they typically aren't as time-consuming, campaign-level and account-level optimizations can be just as important. These optimizations include deciding whether you should adjust bids by placement, adjusting campaign budgets and statuses, reviewing account performance trends, and analyzing changes to margins or fulfillment.

In this chapter, I'll cover a number of higher-level optimizations you can make to drive better performance out of your Amazon ad campaigns. Broadly, these optimizations include bid boosting, changing your campaign budget, and making adjustments due to seasonality.

ADJUSTING BIDS BY PLACEMENT

Because bidding is an ongoing process where the competitive landscape is always changing, it can be difficult to ensure that your bids are high enough to get the top placement without overpaying for clicks and losing control of profitability. Amazon allows you to adjust the bidding strategy (i.e., increase bids for certain placements).

You can enable these advanced bidding strategies in the campaign settings of any manual Sponsored Products campaign. See Figure 15–1 below for an example of what it looks like in the interface.

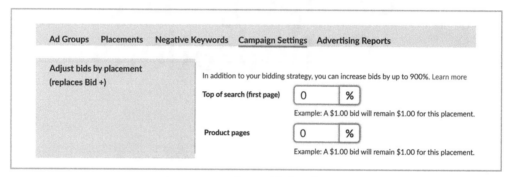

FIGURE 15–1. Adjust Bids by Placement

We recommend adjusting bids by placement for your top-performing manual campaigns as well as any campaigns in which you want to bid more aggressively either on top of search placements or on product detail pages.

ADJUSTING CAMPAIGN BUDGETS AND CAMPAIGN STATUS

Regardless of your brand's investment in advertising on Amazon, you will need to regularly adjust your campaign budgets. Even accounts that are spending the maximum daily budget will still need to make adjustments. If you are working under strict budget constraints, it will be more a matter of reallocating spend within the account than simply increasing or decreasing budgets based on individual campaign performance.

If one of your top-performing campaigns is hitting its budget limit every day, you should increase its budget to make sure those ads can run for the entire day. The last thing you want is to put your time and energy into building a killer campaign only to have it run for just a few hours a day before maxing out its budget. Amazon will display an alert at the top of the Campaign Manager interface whenever one of your campaigns hits its daily budget limit.

One way to check whether your budgets are adequate is to take the average daily spend for each campaign and compare it to their daily budgets. We recommend setting the daily budget about 20 to 40 percent higher than the average daily spend so your campaigns have room to grow. This cushion can be increased during times of peak seasonality or decreased for campaigns with an objective other than profitable growth (e.g., brand awareness).

In addition to adjusting your daily budgets, you can also change your campaigns' duration and status. If you need to set an end date, pause, or archive a campaign, you can do so in its Campaign Settings section.

REVIEWING HISTORICAL TRENDS IN PERFORMANCE

Although it can be tempting to get buried in the weeds, doing keyword research, bid changes, and the like, it is equally important to take a step back and look at your account's overall performance. You should periodically review account performance trends over time to see if you are accomplishing the goals and objectives you set for the account.

While Amazon now allows you to select dates in both Seller Central and Vendor Central, making it easier to see ad performance over a specific date range, users can only view the past 90 days. The interface is also not conducive to viewing trends over time. Although Amazon now provides an interactive graph to show trends for the selected date range, the limited amount of data makes it nearly impossible to analyze quarter-by-quarter and year-over-year trends. Sellers and vendors have come up with some creative workarounds to this problem.

For example, my company works with a well-known brand manufacturer in the toilet and bath fixture industry who was running campaigns in Vendor Central and wanted to compare historical monthly performance. They designed their campaigns to start and end on the first and last day of each month. At the end of the month, they copied all their active campaigns using the copy feature within the Campaign Manager interface, and then updated the start and end dates to reflect the following month.

While this is a popular solution to the Amazon ad interface reporting constraints, campaign history plays a material factor in performance. New campaigns can take several days to ramp up, so pausing and copying the campaigns each month can measurably impact their potential.

At ROI, we have custom software that allows us to review ad performance over time (including keyword and product data). Once the bath manufacturer hired us, we restructured their campaigns to run continuously since we no longer had to worry about keeping track of long-term performance in Amazon's interface. This enabled their campaigns to build history and allowed us to reallocate the time required to copy the campaigns each month to more valuable pursuits, such as advertising additional products and performing keyword research. In their first month, we increased their number of advertised products on Amazon threefold and saw a 126 percent increase in revenue month over month.

Comparing Monthly Performance Past 90 Days

While we have a tool that allows us to see long-term performance at a granular level, you can track advertising performance over time by creating a custom Excel workbook. This will let you compare monthly performance and spot trends at the campaign level. We recommend doing this once the full attribution window is complete for the previous month (seven days in Seller Central and 14 days in Vendor Central). For a refresher on attribution, refer to the Amazon performance data section of Chapter 13. Follow these three steps to create your custom spreadsheet:

1. Before starting to pull the data, set up your master Excel spreadsheet.
   - Label each tab for a specific month so that you have one tab for each month of data.
2. Now you're ready to pull the data.
   - Download one month of campaign data at a time. Select the data range for the previous month in the Campaign Manager (either in Seller Central or Vendor Central), and then export the report to Excel. See Figure 15–2.

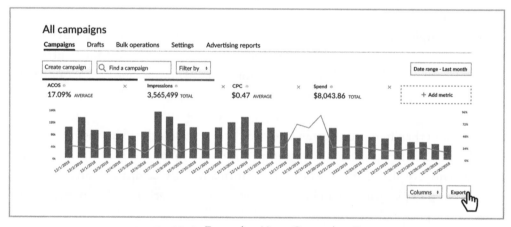

FIGURE 15–2. Exporting Your Campaign Data

3. Once you have pulled the campaign-level data, copy the information to a new tab labeled with the appropriate date in your master spreadsheet.

Each month, review and record the previous month's campaign-level performance data after the full attribution window is complete. Maintaining this Excel file will help you keep track of your historical advertising performance. Although the interface does now include graphs of historic performance, recording the data allows you to have the actual data at your disposal for as far back as you began this process. If your campaigns are structured as outlined earlier, this will also allow you to more easily spot campaign-level trends as well as trends in traffic or keyword type.

When looking at historical performance trends, you should look at the ad's performance as well as your business's performance on Amazon as a whole (including organic sales). By looking at both, you can examine how your advertising strategies are impacting your business. We'll talk more about reviewing performance over time in the next chapter.

ANALYZE IMPACT OF PRIME STATUS CHANGES

When looking at historical performance trends, keep in mind any changes that have been made to fulfillment and how they may have affected performance. For example, if products that were previously Prime-eligible lose the Prime badge, you will likely see advertising performance fall. On the other hand, you will likely see a boost in performance when products gain Prime status.

We recently had a client who saw their performance on Amazon drop drastically once many top products were no longer Prime-eligible. Advertising also lost traction, with fewer impressions, clicks, and sales. We immediately decided to focus advertising spend on the remaining Prime products. This required some pretty heavy lifting in terms of reallocating the budget to ensure we were funneling traffic to those products. Unfortunately, this is essentially the only thing you can do on the advertising side when your products lose Prime status.

If you don't manage the fulfillment piece yourself, I encourage you to work closely with your fulfillment team to learn what steps are necessary to get Prime eligibility for your products. Amazon highly favors Prime products, and if you lose that status, it can be hard to make up the lost ground.

ROTATING ADVERTISED PRODUCTS WITH SEASONALITY

On Amazon, the apparel category can be daunting to navigate, especially with the big brands playing in the space. Therefore, it is extremely important to understand how your products perform at different times of the year and which traffic to go after during those times. For apparel, seasonality is relative to the time of year; therefore, it is crucial to ensure you are aggressively advertising the right products at the right time.

Seasonality is present in almost all categories, and you need to make sure you are in a position to make the most of it. To capitalize on a product's seasonality while still having coverage on the entire product catalog, prioritization is key. This can be accomplished through campaign structure where products are grouped by theme and through implementing a tiered bidding approach.

I work with multiple brands in the fashion apparel space. If you represent a fashion brand, you may have campaigns running for each brand in which all the product styles and keywords being targeted are combined. This type of account structure does not allow you to prioritize seasonal products but instead gives Amazon's algorithm the control over which products to show on certain keywords. When you lose control of your ad campaign, it is more difficult to meet your goals and ensure the customer is seeing the right product.

In Chapter 9 on account structure, I showed you how our company groups similar product types together along with segmenting search traffic. This method allows us to more easily tailor our aggression on certain products and search traffic to, in this case, capture seasonal sales.

Our Amazon advertising team worked with one client on their sportswear collection and started by creating new campaigns by product type: pants, shirts, suits, jeans, and so on. We knew linen products were a focus for spring and a large part of our client's sportswear business, so from a bidding standpoint, we would need to be more aggressive on these products during that season. We took our automatic campaign structure a step further and created separate campaigns around linen pants, linen shorts, linen suits, and linen shirts. By grouping the linen products together and separating them out from the other sportswear products, we could tier our bids, setting higher bids on the linen campaigns to ensure most of our ad spend was funneled to those products.

Using our proprietary tools to find profitable areas of search traffic, we also created manual campaigns focusing on "linen" traffic. Segmenting out this traffic allowed for

AT A GLANCE: A WEEK'S WORK FOR AMAZON ADVERTISERS

Assuming a typical five-day workweek, I have outlined below what a week of adjustments and optimizations should look like for an Amazon advertiser based on my company's best practices.

Monday. If you haven't had a chance to check on your campaigns over the weekend, Monday is a great day to assess performance for the past few days and formulate a plan for scheduled buildouts and optimizations. Any large-scale buildouts of new

AT A GLANCE, continued

campaigns should be front-loaded to the beginning of the week so you can more closely track the initial results of these campaigns through the rest of the week.

Tuesday. Like Monday, Tuesday is a great day to further assess your campaigns' performance but in this case for the entire past week. By this point, most sales data has attributed through the previous Sunday, and you can draw meaningful insights from it. Once you've assessed your performance over the previous week, you can use the rest of Tuesday and Wednesday to conduct any necessary bid optimizations so that when you revisit these optimizations the following week, you will have more complete data with which to analyze and adjust further.

Wednesday. The middle of the week should be when you shoot to have most of your "heavy lifting" buildouts completed. This leaves you ample time to make any further adjustments after the initial results come in. For example, if you are building out a new round of automatic campaigns for products and spend begins to increase at a pace you're not comfortable with, you will want to be able to adjust it before the end of the week to prevent any major problems from happening over the weekend.

Thursday. Typically, Thursday should be the last day you make any large-scale adjustments for the week. By this point, a pretty clear picture of performance from Monday to Wednesday should be forming. This would be a great time to dive into the search term report for the past two to four weeks, add any necessary negative keywords, and bid down or pause any unprofitable keywords.

Friday. Fridays should be reserved as a review day to further analyze performance, plan buildouts for the following week, and assess any other areas of your Amazon strategy apart from advertising. We strongly advise *not* launching any campaigns on Friday that have the potential to capture a high volume of traffic over the weekend unless that is a deliberate strategy for your business. If you plan to enjoy your weekend without accessing your Amazon Advertising account, you do not want to come back to unpleasant results on Monday. Friday is also a great education day: Read some of the countless articles and blogs on Amazon Advertising to ensure you are aware of any large changes coming down the road or any new opportunities your company can take advantage of.

tighter control of our ad spend, and we took advantage of the "linen" search volume while it peaked. For brand terms, we used our tiered bidding approach by setting the client's brand name at a higher bid in the linen brand campaigns than in our other brand campaigns. This approach allowed the linen products to show in top ad spots (although this was also dependent on many other variables).

With this approach, we increased revenue by 62 percent, with just a 56 percent increase in ad spend. We would apply the same process throughout the year, shifting our focus to seasonally relevant products. For example, as fall approaches we would want to decrease aggression on linen and increase it on pants, knits, and sweaters. This constant changing of focus cannot be achieved without a sound campaign structure within which you can implement a tiered bidding approach.

From time to time, you'll want to take a step back and "inspect what you expect." Self-auditing your own account can uncover waste as well as provide insights to grow revenue. In the next chapter, I'll show you what to look for when studying your account for opportunities to improve.

Chapter 16

Self-Auditing

> *Only auditors can save the world—through*
> *peace and reconciliations.*
>
> —ANONYMOUS

Auditing your advertising campaigns (in other words, conducting a critical examination of your campaign structures and settings) can help determine if they are aligned with your business strategies and your goals for advertising on Amazon. It may seem daunting at first, but having a proper campaign structure in place will prove invaluable to your success in advertising on Amazon. In this chapter, we'll outline the most common issues to look for when performing a self-audit on your account.

CREATE A BALANCED AUTOMATIC AND MANUAL CAMPAIGN MIX

First, ask yourself if you are employing a mix of both automatic and manual Sponsored Products campaigns. While it's a popular belief that manual campaigns are more important (because of the clarity and control these campaigns give advertisers), each campaign type serves a different purpose, and it's best to use both automatic and manual campaigns to have full advertising coverage, as seen in Figure 16–1 on page 148.

As mentioned earlier, automatic campaigns provide broad coverage, and manual campaigns are more targeted and typically produce a higher return. It's ideal to include all products you would like to advertise in an automatic campaign—with similar products in the same ad groups—to ensure at least some advertising coverage for them. Since manual campaigns are more targeted, most of your spend should be flowing through them, but employing both ad formats in unison will maximize the amount of traffic to your products.

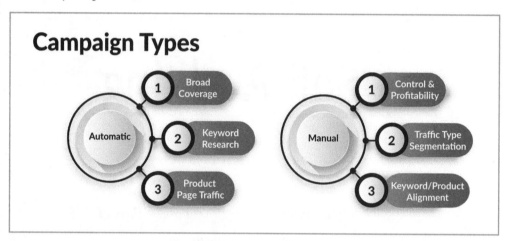

FIGURE 16–1. Campaign Types

There are many other areas you'll want to examine as you audit your campaigns. Let's take a critical look at your campaign structure next.

CHECK FOR STRUCTURE AROUND THE THREE TRAFFIC TYPES

Ask yourself if your campaign is structured in a way that separates the three traffic types: brand, category, and competitor. Creating campaigns that feature keywords specific to one traffic type is essential for clearly understanding the performance of your account. Because brand keywords usually produce a better return, if they are grouped in a campaign with category or competitor keywords, they could artificially drive up the overall revenue of the campaign. Meanwhile, the category keywords may not receive nearly as many impressions. Separating these traffic types is imperative for allocating your ad spend correctly. It also allows you to more easily see how each traffic type is performing.

USE ALL THREE KEYWORD MATCH TYPES

Using all three keyword match types (broad, phrase, and exact) for each keyword in your account is another opportunity to maximize your advertising reach. By implementing broad and phrase match keywords, you could potentially uncover top-converting search queries as keyword opportunities. Most of your spend should ideally flow through exact match keywords since these should be the most relevant keywords with a higher conversion rate. You can achieve this through a tiered bidding structure for each term, with the exact match keyword having the highest bid, followed by phrase match and then broad match.

USE AD FORMATS THAT MAKE SENSE FOR YOUR ADVERTISING STRATEGY

As outlined on page 68, the number of ad formats available to you will depend on whether you are a seller (with our without Brand Registry) or a vendor. It's important to take advantage of all the ad formats that align with your overall goal for advertising on Amazon, as seen in Figure 16–2 below.

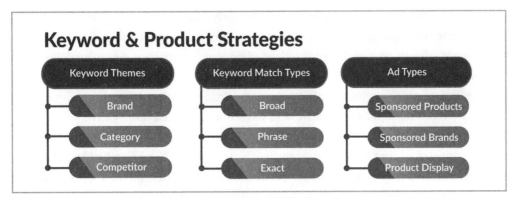

FIGURE 16–2. Keyword and Product Strategies

Sponsored Products for Traffic and Flexibility

As mentioned in Chapter 10, Sponsored Products ads typically produce the most traffic, given the number of placements they receive and given that they have the highest sales per click compared with the other ad formats. I recommend always running Sponsored Products ads, as they can be tailored to any of the three strategies you read about in Chapter 6: brand promotion, rapid growth, and achieving a target ad cost of sale.

Sponsored Brands Campaigns for "Top of Funnel" Growth or Branding

Sponsored Brands campaigns can be a great "top of funnel" or branding opportunity if you are focused on promoting your brand or even growing incremental sales by extending brand reach to new consumers. The prominent banner placement, in addition to having the option of driving traffic to your Amazon Store, is a great brand-awareness opportunity to tell shoppers more about your brand or products. However, since CPC is typically higher than that of Sponsored Products campaigns, due to the limited (but prominent) placements, and since there is a much higher clickthrough rate, Sponsored Brands ads are not as beneficial for achieving a low ACoS metric.

Product Display Ads for Targeting Interests and Product Pages

Similarly, Product Display ads can be another opportunity to inform shoppers about your brand by targeting interests and product pages, including those of your competitors. However, Product Display campaigns should be reserved for strong brand promoters since these are generally the most expensive ad format and typically produce lower attributed sales.

EVALUATE SEARCH QUERY AND PRODUCT AD SPEND

Where is the spend going in your account? Regularly analyzing search queries is essential for knowing how your account is performing. Download a search term report and sort the Spend column to see the highest-spending queries in your Sponsored Products campaigns. This will shed light on what is driving the most spend: brand, category, competitor, or even unrelated traffic. Consider adding unrelated search queries or ones that have received significant traffic and have not converted as negative keywords to prevent wasteful spend. If there are any search queries that convert well and have a lower ACoS, consider adding them as keywords if you do not already have them. Breaking out top-converting search queries as keywords allows you to increase bids and drive additional traffic to terms that have proved to perform well.

Which products are receiving the most ad spend in your account? Since product ad performance can vary from actual product performance on Amazon, it's important to know which products in your campaigns are accumulating the most spend. Review the Advertised Product Report to see product ad performance over the past 60 days for your Sponsored Products campaigns. Based on your business goals, most of the traffic in your account should be going toward your highest-priority products, whether it's your top-performing products to grow sales, products to sell through, or even new-launch products. Consider reducing ad spend for products that do not convert well to improve conversion rates and campaign performance.

IMPLEMENT A STRONG PRODUCT-KEYWORD ALIGNMENT

Are the advertised products aligned with relevant keywords? Review the products and keywords in each ad group throughout your Sponsored Products campaigns. Are there keywords that don't line up with the advertised products? For example, if the targeted keyword is "baseball hat" and baseball gloves are included in the same ad group, consider advertising only baseball hats for stronger product-keyword alignment and increased conversion rates.

Additionally, the optimal product-keyword alignment would feature products with the highest conversion rate for a specific keyword. Continuing with the previous example, align the highest-converting baseball hats for the keyword "baseball hat" in the appropriate ad group. Keep in mind that your top-converting products can vary. For example, the top products for "baseball hat" may be different from the ones for "baseball cap." Product performance can also change over time, so regularly reviewing product ad performance every few months for a specific keyword is imperative for staying on top of trends. Again, you can do this analysis by using the Advertised Product Report. Review the product's performance at the ad level and consider pausing products that have received significant traffic but have not converted. This will reallocate ad spend and traffic to your higher-converting products.

LIMIT KEYWORD DUPLICATION

Are you duplicating keywords across your account? Duplicate keywords throughout the same ad format can lead to inefficiencies in account management and make it difficult to know which products are receiving traffic for a specific keyword. Since keywords across the account will have varying bids, duplicate keywords compete for the same placements, and it's likely that one instance of the keyword will receive more traffic than the others.

Analyze Amazon's Targeting Report for duplicate keywords and consider eliminating the lower-performing ones. In the ideal Sponsored Products campaign structure, outlined in Chapter 10, a keyword is only featured in one ad group within one campaign. A select group of high-priority products that are closely related to the keyword would then be featured in this ad group.

The same is true for Sponsored Brands campaigns. A specific keyword with the same match type should only be included in one campaign. The top related products can then be featured in the banner and on the landing page.

In summary, an internal audit of your account is a great way to give your advertising strategy a real gut check. I recommend conducting these audits at least twice a calendar year and at most once a quarter. They should take no more than a few hours while revealing many strategic gaps and opportunities you can further exploit.

To better keep track of your audit findings, you should create an Excel spreadsheet with tabs dedicated to your high-level insights for each audit pass-through. This can include metrics such as the traffic and ACoS (or TACoS) breakdown of each keyword match type and ad format, your top-performing and worst-performing products, and a calculation of how much spend failed to lead to a conversion.

Keeping track of these key metrics over time will reveal your account's long-term progress toward your KPIs and can serve as a historical footprint for future account managers.

Now that you have your account in a good place, you'll want to do a different kind of prep for peak seasonality (for example, the holiday season). On Amazon, one of the biggest seasonal peaks is the always-popular (and highly profitable) Prime Day.

Chapter 17

Strategies for Amazon's Prime Day

The secret of success is to be ready when your

opportunity comes.

—Unknown

Nothing indicates that a company is fully ingrained in ecommerce consumer culture and behavior quite like inventing a sales holiday in the dog days of summer that ends up raking in more than *$4.1 billion* in global sales in 2018 ($2.6 billion of that U.S.-driven) on a single day. Amazon has done just that with Prime Day. Created in 2015 to celebrate their 20th anniversary as a company, Prime Day offers Amazon Prime subscribers very large discounts on a wide variety of Prime-eligible products. With the exception of 2015, when the first Prime Day fell on a Wednesday, Prime Day has always fallen on the second or third Monday or Tuesday of July.

For 2018's Prime Day, which spanned 36 hours from July 16 to 17, nearly 28 percent of all U.S. online shoppers made at least one purchase on the site. Of these shoppers, 52 percent were first-time Prime Day shoppers, signaling that the explosive growth of this new shopping holiday is far from over.

Needless to say, Prime Day is a huge opportunity for advertisers to promote their products to an eager, high-converting audience. In this chapter, I will discuss the strategies you need to consider to make it a success for your brand and your products.

PRIME ELIGIBILITY AND INVENTORY

The first step to unlocking the growth opportunities Prime Day can deliver is to ensure all your catalog's products are Prime-eligible. The most direct way to achieve this is by sending your inventory to Fulfillment by Amazon (FBA), as discussed in Chapter 1, but depending on your business goals and profit margins, this can prove costly given the various fees Amazon charges for this service. If you have your own fulfillment system that can deliver within Prime's two-day window, your products can become eligible through Seller Fulfilled Prime (a program that allows you to ship to domestic Prime customers with two-day delivery from your own warehouse). You may need to price your products at a premium to cover these shipping costs, but earning Prime eligibility can be more important than listing a price-competitive product without free two-day shipping—especially on Prime Day.

If you have a product or a mix of products you know will convert very well on Prime Day, you will want to ensure you have more than enough inventory set aside to meet the demand, especially since this shopping holiday is considered "out of season" for most brands. Considering that it can sometimes take up to a month for your products to ship, be processed in FBA, and go live on Amazon, you really should start planning for Prime Day in the early spring.

LIGHTNING DEALS AND COUPONS

A Lightning Deal is a "too good to pass up" deal that typically runs in four-hour blocks or until all available items offered on the promotion have been purchased. This can create a situation where certain deals last only *minutes* due to consumer demand. Any product listed with a Lightning Deal can experience a bump in sales and conversions throughout the day, even after the deal has expired. Of course, Amazon charges an extra fee for running Lightning Deals, which increases on high-traffic days such as Prime Day. Within the Lightning Deal interface, your eligible products will automatically populate the product selection window, as you can see in Figure 17–1 on page 155.

Don't expect all your Prime-eligible products to be approved for Lightning Deals—based on their algorithm, Amazon chooses a select number of products with high inventory from each seller's catalog to ensure better visibility for sellers who choose to employ this option.

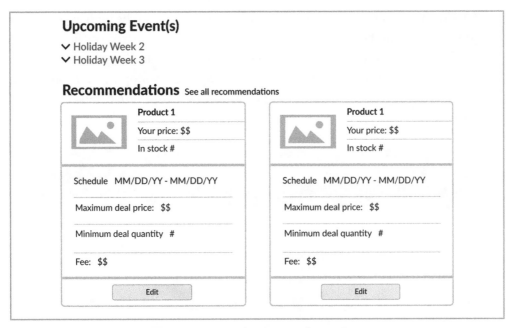

FIGURE 17–1. Lightning Deal Interface

Coupons are also a great way for sellers to push sales on high-traffic days such as Prime Day. Coupon promotions can be accessed under the "Advertising" link in Seller Central. Here you can select products to advertise a coupon for, set their budget, and then activate your coupons, as shown in Figure 17–2.

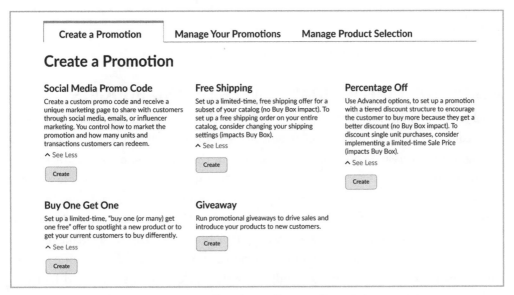

FIGURE 17–2. Creating a Coupon Promotion

Amazon has a 60-cent referral fee for each coupon used, so the budget you set for coupon usage should be based on this metric and your anticipated traffic. Coupons have visibility on these portions of Amazon: product detail pages, the Amazon Coupons page, product search results, email campaigns, shopping carts, and your coupon landing page. Take a look at Figure 17–3 below for more details on coupon page placement.

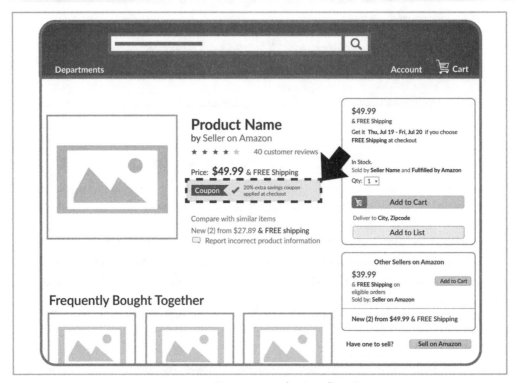

FIGURE 17–3. Coupon on the Landing Page

RIDING THE TRAFFIC TIDAL WAVE: BIDS AND BUDGETS

Much of the planning around Prime Day in terms of fulfillment and discounts will need to be completed and submitted well in advance. Amazon usually releases their due dates for Lightning Deals and coupons in late Q1, and the deliverable dates are anywhere from six weeks to two months prior to Prime Day. The more effective and flexible strategy to ensure Prime Day success will be to optimize your ad campaigns' bids and budgets, based on your business goals and product priorities. This planning is less direct as it requires an element of forecasting and strategic planning that can really make or break your Prime Day performance. If you have seriously underestimated the traffic volume for one of your ads, the campaign budget for that ad can hit its limit and halt very early in the day. Even if you spot this and raise the budget on Prime Day, it can hinder performance as your campaign's visibility and conversion momentum will be starting again from zero.

The same can be said of bids. If you underestimate the rise in CPCs that will most likely occur across your product category on Prime Day, your typically competitive bids may not achieve their usual visibility. Be sure to raise your bids well over the suggested CPC to prevent this.

LAUNCHING SPONSORED BRANDS AND PRODUCT DISPLAY CAMPAIGNS FOR PRIME DAY

In addition to increasing your bids and budgets, you might also want to create new campaigns that highlight your high-priority products (i.e., the products with the best deals, Lightning Deals, discounts, etc.). In addition to the ad copy requirements outlined in Chapter 11, Amazon has further restrictions on the ad copy used in Prime Day Sponsored Brands and Product Display ads. When launching Sponsored Brands or Product Display campaigns specifically for Prime Day, keep in mind a few key requirements:

- You cannot mention "Prime Day" or "Prime members" in the ad copy.
- You cannot target any keywords that include or reference Prime Day.
- Any keywords that do reference Prime Day will direct shoppers to the main Prime Day page rather than to your products.
- As with any non-Prime Day ad copy, you cannot reference any specific pricing promotions (e.g., 20 percent off or $20 off) in the ad copy.
- You cannot include superlatives in your ad copy such as *best in class, best value, biggest savings, highest rated,* or *shopper's top choice.*
- Sponsored Brands and Product Display Prime Day promotional campaigns must have an end date within 24 hours of Prime Day's ending.

If you closely follow these guidelines, your campaigns should be approved by the creative review team and go live before Prime Day traffic begins to pick up. Make sure you submit them for review at least a week before Prime Day in case they are not approved and you need to revise and resubmit.

MEASURING PRIME DAY SUCCESS

After the Prime Day dust has settled and most of your data has been attributed, which can take up to 72 hours, your next task will be to analyze your performance and gain actionable insights by using Amazon's advertising reports. We'll go into more detail about these reports in Chapter 19. For now, I'd suggest looking at a two- to three-day window around Prime Day to get the most out of your data. Here are some useful reports to measure success:

- *Targeting Report.* Through this report, you can gain insights on your best- and worst-performing keywords and which campaigns they drive traffic through.
- *Search Term Report.* With this report, you can go a step further and analyze which customer search terms flowed through those keywords to drive traffic and conversions. This is another great opportunity to check for irrelevant search terms to add as negative keywords later.
- *Advertised Product Report.* This report will reveal which product converted best during this high-traffic period as well as which products had poor performance.
- *Purchased Product Report (Seller Central Only).* This report reveals which products shoppers converted on after clicking on an ad for a different product in your catalog. This data can help you decide whether a product bundle option would be profitable during the next Prime Day or another high-traffic holiday.

If you were advertising on Amazon during the last Prime Day, you will want to review your performance when planning for the upcoming Prime Day. Although the competitive landscape will certainly have changed over the past year, last year's Prime Day performance can be a good indicator of how your products will perform. Using the reports described above, you can decide which products you want to push as well as which products and categories typically do not perform as well. Although Prime Day is undoubtedly a major day for anyone selling on Amazon, the traffic increase does not always translate to higher sales and revenue. The most important thing to consider when deciding how aggressive to be on Prime Day is your brand's historical performance and competitiveness.

CONTINGENCY PLANS AND READJUSTING FOR POST-PRIME DAY

In many cases, the optimizations made to capture sales on Prime Day are too aggressive for average traffic flow and conversion rates during the summer. Make sure to keep a detailed tab on your adjustments so you can return your bids and budgets back to normal levels. The most efficient way is to make most of your adjustments through a bulk upload (covered in the Sponsored Products data analysis section of Chapter 13). This way you have a detailed road map of the exact adjustments made and where they live within the account. Before making these adjustments for Prime Day, I would also **strongly** suggest you complete a bulk download of your account. The bulk download takes a snapshot of your current campaign structure, bids, budgets, and paused or

PRIME DAY CHECKLIST

- Ensure your products are Prime-eligible

- Make sure you have sufficient inventory set aside for Prime Day

- Submit products for Lightning Deals and consider creating coupons for products

- Optimize your campaign bids and budgets to prepare for the influx of competition and traffic on Prime Day

- Launch Sponsored Brands and Product Display campaigns specifically for the priority products you want to push on Prime Day

unpaused products and campaigns. Think of it as an account time machine—if you'd like to immediately return to pre-Prime Day levels, this could be your best bet. In the unlikely event that you had especially poor Prime Day results due to misaligned category expectations or overly aggressive bids and budgets, the bulk download option could be a lifesaver.

USING PRIME DAY DATA FOR LONG-TERM PLANNING

For many brands, the fourth quarter of the calendar year drives a sizable amount of volume (it's the biggest quarter for retail sales in the United States) and can draw the line between a successful year or a poor one. The months between October and December (the holiday season) include Halloween, Thanksgiving, Hanukkah, Kwanzaa, and Christmas.

When prepping for peak seasonality for your product category, whether in Q4 or any other time of the year, your Prime Day data can be an essential asset for informing your product priorities, budgeting, and bidding strategies. That's because for most consumer brands that sell on Amazon, it's the only high-traffic period outside the fourth quarter where you can test products (against competitors), budgets (because the traffic is so high), and promotions. Be sure to securely save your Prime Day statistics to refer to during this prep time. Performance and expectations during high seasonality can be wide-ranging depending on your product category, but there are a few principles and best practices that apply to all categories.

With your strategies for peak seasonality and Prime Day in mind, you're now at a point where you can put all the things you've learned about strategy, structure, and optimization into practice.

In the past several chapters, I've focused almost entirely on Amazon Sponsored ad units (Sponsored Products, Sponsored Brands, and Product Display ads). In the next chapter, you'll learn about a demand-side platform (a system connecting buyers of digital advertising with multiple ad exchanges through one interface) that allows you to programmatically reach your audiences on Amazon websites, apps, and Amazon's publishing partners, and third-party ad exchanges.

Chapter 18

Extending Your Reach On and Off Amazon

We want consumers to say, 'That's a hell of a product'
instead of, 'That's a hell of an ad.'

—LEO BURNETT, AMERICAN ADVERTISING EXECUTIVE (1891–1971)

Now that you have read about all the ins and outs of Amazon search advertising (advertising on Amazon through Sponsored Products, Sponsored Brands, and/or Product Display ads), you can explore some other ways to leverage your presence on Amazon. Some of the most significant opportunities to extend your reach on and off Amazon include participating in Amazon's demand-side platform, Amazon DSP (formerly referred to as AAP); driving off-site traffic to your Amazon Store; and advertising books on Amazon.

AMAZON DSP

Amazon DSP is a demand-side platform, meaning that brands can target shoppers in real time as they browse the internet. This approach allows brands to reach customers on and off Amazon through programmatic display advertisements. You may have heard about this service before through your Amazon representative, as it has been a recent push for

Amazon. If this is your first time hearing about it, get ready because we are about to introduce a whole new world of Amazon advertising.

Through Amazon DSP, Amazon can partner with third-party sites to place ads across the internet. Because these ads can show on Amazon and on other sites, brands can exponentially increase their reach through Amazon DSP. These ads can show in the following placements: desktop and mobile web display ads, mobile banner ads, mobile interstitial ads, and video ads.

This form of advertising can currently be managed either by Amazon or by an agency that has been granted access to the self-service version of Amazon DSP. My company has run ads through Amazon DSP for our clients, and we have seen firsthand the drastic impact this extended reach can have on a company's brand awareness and growth. We have also worked with brands that are running ads in Amazon DSP through the team at Amazon, and we have heard success stories from them as well. The key is to make sure your strategies in Seller Central or Vendor Central are aligned with those in Amazon DSP to maintain a consistent brand message.

This option might be a great opportunity for you if your brand is awareness-driven and you value the reach of your ads over the initial return. This is not to say you won't see a return from your advertising efforts through Amazon DSP, but your expectations should be much different from your expectations of your search advertising efforts. Search advertising aims to increase awareness and sales from people who are already searching on Amazon for products like yours and are therefore likely to convert. With DSP, you can reach customers throughout the purchase cycle using a variety of retargeting and programmatic display methods. You may be targeting a customer who is very early in the research process, who was a cart abandoner on your website, or who is of a certain demographic that is of interest to you and your brand. Targeting based on demographics or interests will lend itself to more of a brand-awareness play.

My company has used DSP to help our clients primarily in two ways: programmatic display ads and retargeting ads. Through programmatic display ads, brands can reach a larger audience both on and off Amazon by targeting specific audiences and segments with real-time bidding. Brands can also use DSP to reengage site/page visitors, cart abandoners, and past purchasers by placing pixels on their own websites to track the customers. Amazon Advertising can also track and engage customers based on the ASINs they viewed and/or purchased on Amazon.

Now let's look more closely at programmatic display and retargeting ads in DSP.

Programmatic Display Strategies

Amazon DSP allows advertisers to target various audiences on and off Amazon through Amazon-exclusive sites (Amazon and IMDB), Amazon Publisher Services, and open exchanges such as AppNexus, Rubicon, and OpenX. You can build audiences to target using Amazon's first-party data, which provides insights into shopping behaviors on Amazon-owned and -operated properties.

Additionally, you can target specific segments of shoppers. For example, if your brand sells high-end purses, you might want to target the fashionista lifestyle segment or the health, beauty, and fashion in market segment. The types of segments available to target include:

- *In market*: Customers who are browsing in a specific market (e.g., parents shopping for baby products)
- *Lifestyle*: Customers who are in broad categories based on their interests (e.g., pet lovers)
- *Demographic*: Customers who fall into specific categories based on their characteristics (e.g., age, gender, income, etc.)

You can layer multiple segments on top of each other to create a unique targeting approach. Within the DSP interface, you can also see the estimated reach of each segment defined in terms of estimated number of impressions per day.

Retargeting Strategies

DSP also allows you to retarget shoppers who have visited your website or viewed your products on Amazon. You can reach and reengage existing customers through pixel and ASIN retargeting. With pixel retargeting, you can track your customers with pixels that are placed on your brand's website and linked to your DSP account; you can then follow customers on and off Amazon to show them ads for your product. ASIN retargeting is similar to pixel retargeting in that you can target existing customers off Amazon, but instead of tracking them via a pixel on your website, you are tracking them from their initial viewing of your product detail page on Amazon. In our experience, ASIN retargeting is not always available via DSP, so speak with your agency or Amazon Advertising representative to see if you can retarget ASINs.

There are a variety of ways to use DSP's retargeting capabilities to grow brand awareness and increase sales. Some of the most common retargeting strategies include:

- *Targeting cart abandoners*: Reengage site visitors who added a product to their cart but did not purchase the product within a specific time frame
- *Cross selling*: Target previous purchasers or site visitors by promoting complementary products or new versions of products
- *Increasing brand awareness*: Reengage previous site visitors to promote brand value and influence them using calls to action

- *Highlighting new product launches*: Target previous purchasers or site visitors and announce a new product they may also be interested in
- *Reminders for renewals*: Reengage previous customers when the product they purchased is at the end of its life cycle, and remind them they will need to purchase again soon

You can try any one or a combination of these to bump up your brand's profile, which will hopefully lead to increased sales.

Amazon DSP Data and Supply Sources

Amazon uses their first-party data to target specific consumers based on their shopping behaviors and interests. You can build off this data by adding any data you have on your existing customers through email lists.

There are three primary supply sources Amazon allows you to choose from when setting up your ads on DSP. You can have your ads run on Amazon-owned and -operated sites, Amazon Publisher Services, and/or open exchanges. Amazon-owned and -operated sites include Amazon and IMDb. Amazon Publisher Services consists of direct publisher inventory for high-visibility impressions. Open exchanges are real-time bidding exchanges, including sources such as AppNexus, Rubicon, and OpenX.

Running Flights in Amazon DSP

When it comes to thinking about your ads in Amazon DSP, you will need to take a step back from everything we've said about Seller Central and Vendor Central account structure. The account structure in DSP is different from what you may be used to with other ad formats. In Seller Central and Vendor Central we create campaigns and then ad groups at the next level. DSP has orders and then line items at the next level. If you are just starting in DSP, it can be helpful to think about orders as campaigns and line items as ad groups.

Table 18–1 below is a visual representation of the structure of Amazon DSP:

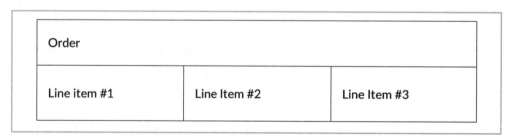

Order		
Line item #1	Line Item #2	Line Item #3

TABLE 18–1. Structure of Amazon DSP Orders

The order is the overarching level that defines the ultimate start and end dates, total budget, and conversion tracking. The line items are where you will define the targeting (supply sources, frequency, etc.), segments, bids, and optimization types. You can have multiple line items running simultaneously for the same order.

It is considered best practice to separate supply sources at either the order or line item level depending on how granular you want to get. Placements on Amazon-owned and -operated sites will perform differently from placements on an open exchange site, so you should have separate orders or line items for each supply source you are using. You will also likely want to set different bids and budgets for each supply source, which is another good reason to separate them.

Earlier in this book, we discussed running campaigns continuously in Seller Central and Vendor Central. Another difference when it comes to advertising in Amazon DSP is that orders are run in flights rather than being run continuously. Flights are essentially orders and line items that will run for a predetermined time frame to execute the desired strategy. In fact, Amazon DSP requires a specified end date for all orders. You can choose any time period, but typically, you will want to run flights for 60 or 90 days at a time.

Once a flight has ended, take any learnings from it and use them when creating a new flight. In Seller Central and Vendor Central you mostly make optimizations within existing campaigns. However, optimizations in DSP work best when implemented from one flight to the next.

There are a handful of optimizations you might want to make while a flight is still running, such as adjusting bids, applying a catch-up boost, and possibly even excluding poor-performing creative sizes or website placements. Keep in mind that any changes to the flight will impact the algorithm and performance until it can adjust—typically a few days. For example, if you pause poor-performing creatives in the middle of the flight, overall performance will likely decrease until the algorithm can adjust to the changes. Any major changes or optimizations should be made in between flights to avoid a major dip in performance.

Creative Assets for DSP

When setting up creatives, you will need to create them and then assign them at the line item level. You can upload the following types of creatives in DSP:

- Video
- Image (standard, mobile DSP, and mobile owned and operated)
- Dynamic ecommerce (standard, mobile DSP, and mobile owned and operated)
- Flash
- Third party (standard, mobile DSP, and video)

You can copy creatives and then revise them when setting up multiple creatives. To do this, just click the copy button under the first creative you set up. This should save you time as you set up your line items and creatives.

DRIVING OFF-AMAZON TRAFFIC TO YOUR AMAZON STORE

In the past, many clients have come to us wanting to send traffic from other sites, especially social media sites, to their products on Amazon. Until recently, there was no way to track the sales that would have come from these ads. But now, with the metrics available from Amazon Stores, you can see the daily visitors, views per visitor, sales, and units sold.

Essentially, you can now send traffic from other websites to your Amazon Store and track the visitors, sales, and units sold through your store from specific tagged sources. The metrics available through your Amazon Store can be broken out as:

- *Daily visitors*: The total number of users who viewed at least one of your store's pages in a day
- *Views per visitor*: The average number of pages a user views in a day
- *Sales*: The estimated total sales from users within 14 days of their most recent visit to your store
- *Units sold*: The estimated total number of units bought by users within 14 days of their most recent visit to your store

You can see each of these metrics for traffic from Sponsored Brands campaigns, organic traffic to your store, and tagged sources. The tagged sources allow you to connect the dots between the off-Amazon traffic and the traffic to your store. You can tag sources on Amazon through the Amazon Stores Insights page by clicking on "Create Source Tag." Then you'll give that tag a name and generate a link. Once you have created your tags, you can see how each tagged source performs when directed to your Amazon Store.

Let's look at an example of what this might look like for a brand that is interested in sending traffic from their Facebook ads to their Amazon Store for an upcoming Fourth of July sale. First, make sure you have your Amazon Store properly set up and live on Amazon. Also make sure your Facebook ad is set up and ready to run. Next, create a source tag in the Amazon Store interface. This will generate a tag that can be added to the targeted URL. Give your source tag a name that clearly states its strategy/objective. In this example, you might choose "Facebook July 4th Sale." Once the Facebook ad has been launched and is driving traffic to your store, you will begin to see the metrics come in on Amazon.

It is important to note that you can only see metrics for traffic that is directed to your store. At this time, there is no reliable way to track the performance of off-Amazon traffic driven to specific product detail pages. However, this is still a significant improvement in that some traffic can now be tracked from off-Amazon placements.

If you would still rather send traffic to a specific product detail page instead of your Amazon Store, there is a way to make your store more relevant to the traffic being sent from other sites. One strategy our clients have used is to ensure that they constantly update their Amazon Store to include the most up-to-date product releases, promotions, seasonal ad copy, etc. If you are really set on sending traffic to one specific product but still want to be able to see the metrics from Amazon, consider making that product the first thing customers see on your Amazon Store. That way, you can increase the chance that consumers will click on it.

ADVERTISEMENTS FOR BOOKS

If you are a book publisher and a vendor on Amazon, you are in luck because books have a couple of additional campaign opportunities. The first is a Custom Text Sponsored Products ad. This ad format is a Sponsored Products campaign that features one product per campaign and allows for up to 150 characters of customizable text. Since these are PPC ads, having an enticing text description of the book could help improve the conversion rate once a shopper clicks on the ad.

In addition, Kindle e-books have an additional ad format available for vendors: Lock Screen ads. These interest-based PPC campaigns serve advertisements that are featured in various placements on the Kindle, including lock screens and home screens. Amazon provides a set list of reader-related interests to choose from, so be sure to select interests that are relevant to your title.

Unlike Amazon's other campaign formats, you must select a start and end date, and campaigns can only run up to six months at a time. Budgets are also slightly different in that you cannot select a daily budget but rather assign an overall budget for the campaign. You can, however, spread the budget evenly across the duration of the campaign or spend it as quickly as possible. You can also increase the budget during the campaign if you choose, but it must be above the $100 minimum.

Similar to the Custom Text Sponsored Products ads, advertisers can feature one title per Lock Screen campaign along with up to 150 characters of customizable text. Again, this allows you to provide further detail about the advertised book and can help improve clickthrough and conversion rates.

While Amazon DSP can extend your ads both on and off Amazon, I would be doing you a disservice if I did not cover how to think about the way your Amazon advertising fits into the bigger picture and how to present this to your brand's executives, whether they're members of a large board or your own small team of owners (even if that's just you and a spouse).

In our final chapters, we will discuss how to report to executives on Amazon performance, how to decide if an agency is right for you, and the importance of a customer-centered mindset on Amazon.

Chapter 19

Reporting for Executives

As a general rule the most successful man in life is the man who has the best information.

—BENJAMIN DISRAELI, BRITISH STATESMAN (1804–1881)

The data that advertisers gather on Amazon can be very different from the data an executive would like to use when formulating a business decision. Where in-the-trenches marketers may be more concerned with the day-to-day performance of specific high-volume keywords, the optimum mix of products to be advertised, or the best ad format(s) for a given category, executives want more high-level information about their brand's performance in the channel over time.

Ideally, the data executives want from Amazon could still be broken down on a granular level, but that is currently difficult because it is not organized in a central location where you can easily pull and digest it.

In this chapter, I will outline the business reports that are readily available in Amazon's interface and how to use them to drive further advertising insights for your company's executives.

BUSINESS REPORTS IN VENDOR CENTRAL

If you are a vendor to Amazon, the process of gathering this account-level data will be much less direct than it is through Seller Central. This is because in a vendor relationship, Amazon holds title to the inventory it has purchased from a brand. Once Amazon owns the inventory, they can sell and track it any way they wish without providing any reporting back to the brand. But because Amazon also wants brands to invest in advertising on the site, the incentive to provide more data to vendors will continue to rise.

For vendors, data on total Amazon sales and purchase orders from Amazon is found in the Amazon Retail Analytics section of Vendor Central and may be available only upon request from your Amazon category manager. There is a premium version of this report that delivers even deeper insights, but it commands a significant fee ($35,000 per year as of this writing).

Since business-level reports are not as easily accessible through Vendor Central as through Seller Central, we will not focus on the reports Amazon must provide for you via category manager or Retail Analytics as these can vary by situation.

BUSINESS REPORTS IN SELLER CENTRAL

The most direct way for executives to find high-level performance metrics in Seller Central is to go to the "Reports" link and then select "Business Reports," as shown in Figure 19–1.

There are three main report types in the Business Reports section: the Sales Dashboard, the Sales and Traffic Report, and the Detail Page Sales and Traffic Report by ASIN. Refer to Figures 19–2, 19–3, and 19–4, on pages 170 through 172, to see the corresponding report types. Most of the reports in this interface can also pivot from an over-time view of data to a by-product presentation. Next we'll look at a more detailed breakdown of the reports.

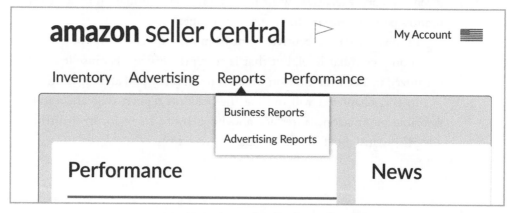

FIGURE 19–1. Accessing Business Reports

Sales Dashboard

This dashboard provides a daily snapshot of performance data for sales and units ordered alongside a graphical view of orders and sales with a trend comparison across previous day, week, and year performance.

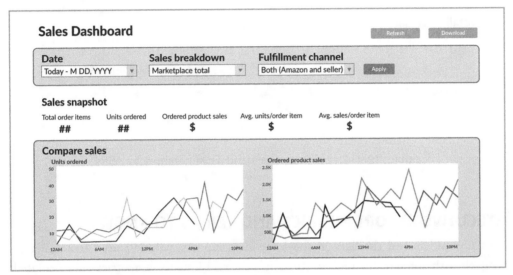

FIGURE 19–2. Sales Dashboard

Sales and Traffic Report

This report aggregates account-level sales and order metrics along with total sessions on a daily, weekly, or monthly basis. Along with all other business reports in Seller Central, it provides a lookback window of up to two years.

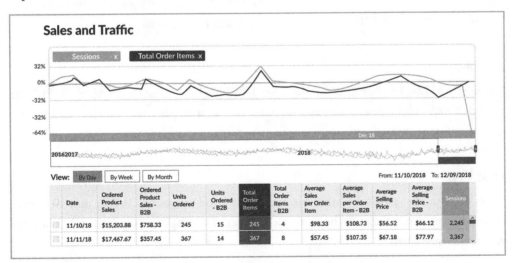

FIGURE 19–3. Sales and Traffic Report

Detail Page Sales and Traffic Report by ASIN

This report breaks down sales and traffic at the ASIN level for a customizable period of time. This is the deepest level of granularity Amazon provides at the business reporting level concerning individual product performance.

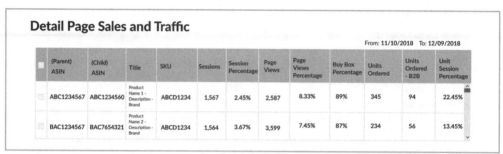

FIGURE 19–4. Detail Page Sales and Traffic Report by ASIN

EXECUTIVE REPORT METRICS AND TERMS TO KNOW

To truly understand the data in these business reports, you will need to familiarize yourself with some of the metrics Amazon uses and how those metrics are calculated. Here are some terms you must know for these reports.

Parent and Child ASINs

Parent and child ASINs are assigned to any product that has a variation option on the product detail page. The parent ASIN is always the one listed in the URL when first clicking on a product detail page. The parent ASIN is usually assigned to the bestselling version, and the child ASINs are assigned to all other variations.

Sessions

Sessions are visits to your Amazon product detail pages by a customer within a 24-hour period. A user might view your pages many times on a single visit, resulting in a higher number of page views than sessions in your reports.

Page Views

Visits to your offer pages during a selected time period (a session). A user may view your offer pages multiple times within a single session, resulting in a higher number of page views than sessions.

Buy Box Percentage

The percentage of page views where the buy box (the "Add to Shopping Cart" link) appeared on the page for customers to add your product to their cart. This percentage will be less than 100 percent if the page view occurred when:

- The product was out of stock.
- The buy box was controlled for a time by another seller on the listing.

Ordered Product Sales: B2B

The amount of ordered product sales from business buyers (determined by multiplying the price of the ordered items by the number of units sold for the selected time period). Amazon defines "business buyers" as sellers who are enrolled in the Amazon Business program who may have access to wholesale discounts exclusive to the program.

Average Units Per Order Item

Determined by dividing the units ordered by the total order items. For example, 7 dog leashes divided by 2 order items is an average of 3.5 units per order item.

Order Session Percentage

The number of orders that were generated relative to the number of customers who viewed the products. This is calculated by dividing the number of orders by the number of sessions for a selected time period.

REPORTING RESOURCES ON AMAZON: FIND AND COMBINE

Due to the lack of "ready to use" reporting in the Amazon interface, you will need to combine data points from various resources to piece together a true picture of your business' current performance on Amazon. On Seller Central, this process is fairly straightforward if you know your way around Excel and can combine data sets that share unique identifiers, such as ASINs. For example, if you wanted to compile data charting your product catalog performance at both the ad level and the organic level, you would need to use the Detail Page Sales and Traffic Report by ASIN (as shown in Figure 19-4 on page 172) in the Business Reports section of Seller Central and the Advertised Product Report within the Advertising Reports section. With these two reports pulled for the same time frame, you can compile and compare sales and spend metrics at the ASIN level with the organic performance of those ASINs. See Figure 19-5 on page 174.

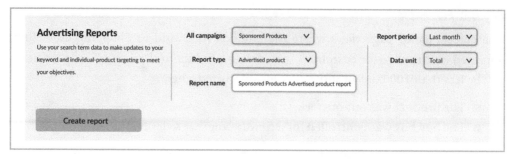

FIGURE 19–5. Advertised Product Report

COMMON BUSINESS-LEVEL KPIS TO CALCULATE

Business-level reports are a valuable tool not only for identifying opportunities that can inform your advertising strategy, but also for providing clarity on overall channel performance for executives. Following are some KPIs and metrics my team and I have used to analyze data for our clients and their executive teams. You've already read about some of these, but they are worth mentioning again here in the context of how you can present them in an executive report.

Advertising Cost of Sales (ACoS)

Equation: Ad Spend ÷ Ad Revenue

Where to find: Amazon calculates ACoS in both the Vendor Central and Seller Central ad interfaces. To calculate an ACoS for all your campaigns, refer to the interface or go to the Targeting Report total up the Spend and Sales columns, and divide. The Advertised Product Report and Search Term Report work as well, but we have observed some small attribution discrepancies.

Insights: As Amazon's preferred method of delivering campaign and keyword profitability data, it's important to know this metric and its ranges at the account level, the product category, and the traffic segment level.

Total Advertising Cost of Sales (TACoS) (Third-Party Sellers Only)

Equation: Ad Spend ÷ Total Amazon Revenue

Where to find: To calculate this metric, you will first need to total your ad spend for a fixed period in the same way described above. Then you will need to go to the Detail Page Sales and Traffic Report by ASIN in the Business Reports section of Seller Central. Through the same fixed window, you will want to total up your Ordered Product Sales column; this will be your denominator.

Insights: This number takes your account ACoS and expands it to a more global level of analysis. Gauging what percentage of total revenue your ad spend currently stands at can help unlock growth opportunities and further contextualize your ad efforts for colleagues or executives looking to analyze profitability in multiple channels.

ROAS (Return on Ad Spend)

Equation: Ad Revenue ÷ Ad Spend

Where to find: This metric is easy to calculate via the Targeting, Search Term, or Advertised Product Report in both the Vendor Central and Seller Central ad interfaces. Amazon has also begun to roll out this metric in many of its reports on a per-ASIN or per-campaign basis.

Insights: ROAS is another angle from which to measure profitability. Since ROAS is a much more common metric than ACoS in the paid search and digital marketing landscape, it's useful to have this calculation handy when discussing your Amazon ad performance across channels.

Cost Per Acquisition (CPA)

Equation: Ad Spend ÷ Orders

Where to find: You can calculate this metric by again referring to any of the three ad reports mentioned above and totaling and dividing the Spend and Orders columns. Be sure to only total orders driven by your ads, not business-level orders, to get an accurate measurement.

Insights: This measures the aggregate cost to acquire a shopper on a campaign, traffic segment, or channel level. This KPI is great for measuring the effectiveness of campaigns and their underlying strategies. Establishing a desired CPA range can drive both profitability and targeted reach.

Clickthrough Rate (CTR)

Equation: Clicks ÷ Impressions

Where to find: CTR is a metric available in both the Search Term and Targeting Reports for vendors and sellers. The metric is also an option within the Seller Central interface. In the reports, the metric is on a per-keyword or per-search-term basis. To calculate a total CTR, you will need to total the Clicks and Impressions columns and then divide.

Insights: CTR is a great way to gauge the effectiveness of ads, their content, and the keywords driving those ads. Campaigns, keywords, or ASINs with an especially low CTR could indicate poor product-keyword alignment or reveal unprofitable search-term traffic to avoid.

Average Order Value (AOV)

Equation: Revenue ÷ Orders

Where to find: The metrics for this calculation can be found in the Search Term, Targeting, and Advertised Product Reports. For a business-level calculation in Seller Central, you can use the same metrics within the Detail Page Sales and Traffic Report by ASIN.

Insights: Calculating AOV at the account, product category, and traffic segment levels unlocks many insights concerning the changes in customer order size over time. If you are testing product mixes, a bundle option, or introducing a bulk ASIN, you will want to pay special attention to your AOV and how it changes after these strategic introductions.

Ad Conversion Rate (Conversion Rate)

Equation: Orders ÷ Clicks

Where to find: Conversion rate is available at the account level within the Seller Central interface and is also listed in the Search Term, Targeting, and Advertised Product Reports on both the keyword and ASIN level. To calculate a total ad conversion rate for a fixed period, you will need to total up the Orders and Clicks columns for one of the reports mentioned above and then divide.

Insights: Knowing your conversion rate at the account, product category, and traffic segment levels is paramount to understanding your product catalog's place in Amazon's ad ecosystem and competitive landscape. If your conversion rates are especially low or have dropped, it may be time to improve your listing pages, clean up your product ratings, and check on your competitors' product options. You may also want to ensure that the product showing for certain keywords with low conversion rates is the most relevant.

Organic Conversion Rate (Third-Party Sellers Only)

Equation: Total Order Items ÷ Sessions

Where to find: Your total Amazon conversion rate can be found in the Detail Page Sales and Traffic Report by ASIN within Seller Central's Business Reports section.

Insights: Calculating your global Amazon conversion rate at the ASIN and product catalog level can provide even more context for your advertising, listing optimization, and product launch efforts. Tracking your global Amazon conversion rate over time can shed light on buying patterns, category seasonality, and the effects of price changes.

Percent of Sales New-to-Brand

Equation: New-to-brand revenue ÷ ad revenue

Where to find: The new to brand revenue (sales) and ad revenue (sales) can be found in Seller and Vendor Central Campaign Manager.

Insights: Analyzing your percent of sales that are from new customers can provide insight into how many new customers your ads are bringing in for the business. Sales are considered new-to-brand if the shopper has not purchased a product from your brand within the past 12 months. The new-to-brand data is a recent release from Amazon, and data only goes back to November 1, 2018 (any earlier time frame will calculate these metrics using November 1 as the start date). Additionally, new-to-brand data is only available for Sponsored Brands and Amazon DSP at this time.

Once you've provided the reporting your executives need to make top-level decisions that affect your overall Amazon ad strategy, the pressure to take it up a few notches will get even more intense. Perhaps you'll need an outside partner to do the heavy lifting for you. In our next chapter, I'll outline how and when to bring in some outside help.

Chapter 20

Hiring an
Advertising Agency

> *Hire people who are better than you are, then leave them to*
> *get on with it. Look for people who will aim for the*
> *remarkable, who will not settle for the routine.*
>
> —DAVID OGILVY, ADVERTISING PIONEER AND FOUNDER OF OGILVY & MATHER (1911–1999)

Amazon campaign management shouldn't be an add-on task for existing members of your sales or marketing team. Brands have too much to lose by thinking of Amazon advertising as a checklist duty. While this can work when you are just getting started, once you have a significant volume of Amazon sales revenue (typically at least six figures a month), having top talent and expertise in this domain accelerates your growth and impacts the dynamics of your business as a whole.

A few years ago, my property manager and I met with three men from the project management division of CBRE here in Raleigh to talk about the upfit of our new building for ROI Revolution to take place in early 2017.

Right away the regional guy asked me a great question: "Timothy, what are you looking for in a project management company? What's your biggest concern?" I said, "Ultimately, I'm looking for a company that is smart and gets things done."

I added that expertise in their core area (in this case, project management for a significant facility upfit) was a given; all three had *years* of experience in project management. What wasn't a given was the degree to which they were uniquely gifted for the role and the degree of their internal drive and motivation.

Once you reach a significant volume on Amazon, the realities of growth are that you'll need abundant access to three key ingredients: time, tools, and expertise. You can hire staff, acquire tools, and build the expertise over time, or you can short-cut the staffing and learning process by hiring an agency to grow your brand for you with Amazon advertising.

In this chapter, I'll cover how to free yourself up with the help of an outside agency with strong Amazon advertising chops.

IS AN AGENCY THE RIGHT OPTION FOR MY BRAND? THREE QUESTIONS TO ASK

Let's pause for a quick reality check. Regardless of the virtues of agency management, it may *not* be a good idea to hire an agency for your brand. Before considering the matter further, assess where you stand by answering three questions:

How Much Revenue Am I Generating from Amazon Sales Each Month?

Every brand starts somewhere. Though well-known brands and highly capitalized ventures have been known to hit their annualized revenue targets on Amazon almost immediately, the path to success is more iterative for most brands.

Advertising can certainly accelerate your growth on Amazon, especially through its ability to kick-start new product sales. Even so, an agency is not a silver bullet to success on Amazon. Success is ultimately driven by a strong brand, a solid business model, tight operations, and sufficient capital.

Agency management typically costs at least a few thousand dollars per month *before* advertising fees. So before enlisting an agency with Amazon Advertising specialists, it's a good idea to wait until your brand is driving at least six figures in monthly Amazon revenue with sufficient profitability. Consult the strategies in this book to help get you there!

Am I the Brand Owner?

Amazon advertising campaigns are available to brands and resellers (first- and third-party sellers) alike. That said, resellers are at a disadvantage when it comes to the economics of advertising. There are two main reasons brand owners have an advantage:

1. *Brands enjoy the full organic benefit of advertising.* Amazon only shows your ads when you're winning the buy box, so your advertising will be throttled if you're sharing the buy box with other sellers. You may benefit from sales revenue generated by your ads, but *every* successful sale and product review strengthens the ASIN as a whole. So every seller in buy box rotation enjoys the knock-on organic boost from increased product performance. With this dynamic at play, only brand owners (or sellers with brand exclusivity) reap the full value from advertising.

2. *Brands enjoy healthier product margins.* As a general rule, the upfront costs involved in product manufacturing or private labeling provide brands with lower per-unit costs than resellers can secure for similar products. All things being equal, stronger margins allow brands to bid more for advertising clicks and still remain profitable. Higher bids mean better ad placement and more sales. Resellers, even those with brand exclusivity, don't have as much wiggle room to invest in competitive (and profitable) category-level advertising campaigns after paying Amazon's fees.

Is Amazon Advertising a Core Internal Competency?

As I mentioned earlier in this chapter, redundancy of expertise is *vital*. In-house campaign management only begins providing an operational safety net once you have at least two or three people dedicated to your Amazon advertising. Internal competency, however, involves more than head count. The following considerations also expose the difficulties of taking a campaign in-house.

Focused Commitment and Buy-In

Businesses succeed due to their unique ability to provide value to their market. The most powerful growth lever, whether on an individual or company level, is the honest self-awareness to double down on your strengths and outsource the rest. Many businesses, however talented, could not legitimately include "Amazon advertising" on a list of their unique strengths.

Beardbrand, a men's grooming brand, drives most of their revenue through wholesale and their own website. Amazon had never accounted for much more than 10 percent of their revenue. Beardbrand assumed the best way to stop dabbling and get serious on Amazon was to hire in-house expertise.

This is not a success story.

Months of failed efforts to recruit the right candidate produced nothing but disillusionment and distraction from their core marketing endeavors. In the end, they made the drastic decision to shut down their entire Amazon channel and focus solely on their proven wholesale and website growth efforts. Beardbrand's story is a sober reminder that an unwarranted commitment to in-house management can often be a profit-killing diversion.

Tools and Automation Don't Run the Show

There's no doubt that it is impossible to maintain competitive advertising campaigns through a completely manual process. From prioritizing relevant keywords to determining the ideal bid, the right tools are essential.

Yet without expert human oversight, tools and automation can do little more than maintain a steady state. If your goal is growth, set-and-forget just won't cut it. With fierce competition, battle lines and growth opportunities are constantly in flux. Campaign planning and optimization must be ongoing. An expert will choose the right tools for the job, but **the real work is always strategic before it is tactical**.

In summary, an agency with deep Amazon Advertising expertise will provide the most value for brands already driving at least six figures in monthly revenue through Amazon, especially for companies that lack a core internal competency in Amazon Advertising.

WHAT AN AGENCY CAN DO FOR YOU

More than 100 years ago, American writer Elbert Hubbard published a small pamphlet about a little-known war hero, Andrew S. Rowan, during the time of U.S. President William McKinley.

From the pamphlet:

When war broke out between Spain and the United States, it was very necessary to communicate quickly with the leader of the Insurgents. Garcia was somewhere in the mountain fastnesses of Cuba—no one knew where. No mail or telegraph message could reach him. The President must secure his co-operation, and quickly.

What to do!

Some one said to the President, "There is a fellow by the name of Rowan who will find Garcia for you, if anybody can."

Rowan was sent for and given a letter to be delivered to Garcia.

The story goes on to tell how the "fellow by the name of Rowan" took the letter from the president and did not ask "Where is Garcia?" but instead took it, "sealed it up in an oilskin pouch, strapped it over his heart, in four days landed by night off the coast of Cuba from an open boat, disappeared into the jungle, and in three weeks came out on the other side of the Island, having traversed a hostile country on foot, and delivered his letter to Garcia."

This story illustrates that quality that nearly everyone admires yet precious few display: *getting things done*. And perhaps it should be said that the greatest complement to getting things done is getting them done without being asked a second (or third) time. Keep this story in mind when you are deciding whether you should hire an agency or go it alone.

Benefits of Outsourcing to an Agency

You have a department to run, perhaps even an entire business. Free yourself to focus on matters you alone are equipped to handle. You'll thrive to the extent that you're able to offload key work into reliable, skilled hands. Not every task demands Rowan-level proficiency. Such single-minded diligence and capabilities come at a price. Yet for business-critical work requiring specialized skills, the investment is well worth it. Need a new building upfitted in time for your company headquarters' relocation? Put a Rowan on it. Need a competitive advertising campaign to pour rocket fuel on your Amazon sales? You need a Rowan.

Analyst Redundancy

But there's a problem with Rowans. No matter how skilled and well-regarded the individual, it is risky to entrust business-critical competencies to a single person. While there are many ways marketing agencies provide unique value, one of the biggest is *redundancy*. You don't want your entire Amazon marketing strategy and execution to fall apart when your Amazon specialist hands you their two-week notice.

There's too much on the line to rely on one person. If this person is you, there are probably higher-level business growth initiatives you could focus on. Sure, you could hire a rock star. The right agency, however, gives you an entire *team* of rock stars. Multiple minds tackling an issue are always better than one. And when you hire a team, you want one that's been there, done that, and possesses the expertise and institutional knowledge that comes from years of "going deep" in a single niche.

Cutting-Edge Expertise

Great agencies earn their keep not only for their resiliency but also for their expertise. Nothing sharpens an analyst's skills more than working daily with mentors who have cut their teeth on Amazon since day one. It's even better if these mentors are trusted by clients to profitably manage millions of dollars in advertising spend per month across multiple verticals.

Expertise is never one-and-done. Amazon is constantly updating their advertising habitat—sometimes weekly. Some changes are minor, while others can have a transformative impact on advertisers' competitive strategies and tactics. Agencies keep their finger on the pulse, maintaining top-of-mind awareness of the latest developments, features, betas, strategies, and tactics needed to achieve the strongest campaign performance.

Insider Access

Amazon intends for their advertising solutions to be completely self-service. Even so, questions and issues still frequently arise for which no clear solutions can be found. Though vendors and sellers driving revenue at Amazon's highest category tier may be offered an account manager, most aren't operating at the scale required to receive personal attention from Amazon. Online documentation, help forums, and automated feedback channels are typically the only support options available.

But there's a backdoor. A handful of high-volume agencies have made it onto Amazon's radar. These official partner agencies have an inside line of personal support, and their clients can piggyback on that direct access through their agency relationship. There are no guarantees, but in addition to Amazon support, such a connection often provides first-in-line access to powerful new advertising features and invitations to test new betas. It's nice to get an edge!

Efficiency of Operations

The greater the scale of an operation, the greater the internal drive for efficiency. This dynamic is what drives the economy and why retail is profitable at all. (The more widgets you purchase or manufacture, the cheaper the per-unit cost, and the greater your margin.)

Amazon's business is nothing if not efficient. With a profit margin less than a tenth that of Facebook, Amazon must operate with streamlined precision. Amazon makes incredible investments in acquisitions and internal projects designed to drive additional efficiency and increase the value to customers. For example, to reduce fulfillment costs the movements of more than 100,000 robots are carefully coordinated across their global web of warehouses and fulfillment centers.

Agencies earn their keep through this same principle. Through advanced work flows and proprietary technology, specialized agencies tend to operate at a much higher efficiency level than in-house teams. This applies to account management essentials such as campaign buildout, reporting, optimization, and analysis.

Just as it doesn't make economic sense for individual authors to buy their own printing presses, it rarely makes economic sense for individual brands to develop their own cutting-edge ad campaign management systems, tools, and technology integrations. Even when tasked with purely manual work, agencies can speed up rollout by scaling up to "all hands on deck" when warranted.

Yes, advertisers officially have everything they need to build and launch campaigns themselves using Amazon's self-service advertising. Yet out-of-the-box reporting and manual work flows can only take you so far. In highly competitive verticals, campaign optimization efficiency is critical for growth and profitability.

Decreased Overhead and Business Risk

Assuming you have access to a strong vendor, outsourcing is a straightforward way to reduce your risk. There's a good reason some smaller to midsize brands forgo maintaining their own warehouse space and instead contract with Amazon to manage their inventory and order fulfillment. This not only turns the fixed cost of warehouse space and employees into a variable one, but it also allows you to capitalize on Amazon's efficiency.

It's a good strategy to minimize upfront expenses and tie costs to utilization whenever possible. Outsourcing makes a company nimbler on their growth path and better able to respond to changes in capital and cash flow. Even when outsourcing appears more expensive on paper, make sure you are taking into account the liability of acquiring, maintaining, and offloading in-house resources.

For example, it may take six months or more to ramp up your warehouse space and an additional six-plus months to divest yourself of unneeded space. In a similar manner, internal hires require significant time and money for recruiting, onboarding, management, and training. And even successful hires with strong cultural fit and on-the-job performance can leave with virtually no warning. As such, there is obviously considerable risk in hiring an in-house analyst to manage your Amazon campaigns, especially given their central role to your success on Amazon.

There's another great benefit to the decreased overhead that comes from outsourcing: a more attractive income statement, which often leads to higher overall business valuation. This is a strong advantage if your eventual goal is to attract investment and/ or buyers for your business.

FINDING AND CHOOSING THE RIGHT AGENCY: EIGHT QUESTIONS TO ASK

The differences between agencies are far more than just their fees. You'll get the best performance from a trustworthy agency that matches your desires and expectations in areas such as speed and responsiveness, clarity of communication, expertise, fees, and efficiency. While hiring an agency is by no means as taxing and time-consuming as hiring an employee, the process still requires careful due diligence.

Before you can begin reviewing the strengths and weaknesses of individual agencies, you need a list of agencies to research. It's relatively easy to find reputable agencies with more general online marketing expertise, but Amazon Advertising is a much more specialized service with far fewer established players.

Be advised that information found on agency comparison/ranking websites can't be trusted. These tend to operate in the same shady way as most product-comparison sites, with rankings generated in one of two ways: Either the top rank goes to the agency that secretly owns the "third party" website, or the top rankings go to the agencies that pay the website owner the highest fees.

It's useful to have a grid through which you can examine key differences between agencies. The following eight questions will help expose weaknesses in early contenders and give you the confidence to choose the right agency for your business. The answers to some of the questions will require a phone call, but many can be gleaned from the agency's website. Before starting out, make sure you understand the context of each question and how to assess the quality of the answers you get back from each agency.

What Is the Pricing Structure?

Though cost is an obvious factor, it must be weighed in proper context. The difference in fees between a decent agency and a truly great agency with deep Amazon expertise may amount to a few thousand dollars per month. Differences in technology and expertise between those agencies, however, can drive performance one or more orders of magnitude above agency fee discrepancies.

That said, agencies typically price their services in the following ways:

- Fixed fee based on level of service
- Flat fee or percentage of ad spend managed (whichever is greater)
- Flat fee + percentage of advertising-generated revenue

There isn't one "best" way to price agency services. At the end of the day, reputable agencies scale the resources they put into each client's account based on the monthly fee earned. So keep in mind that while lower fees may look better on paper, they almost always signify a lower investment on the agency's part, too.

What Are the Contract Terms and Commitments?

Contract length should be a greater financial consideration than your monthly fee. Even the most expensive agency fees can be justified by strong performance, but what happens if the performance isn't there? What a nightmare to find yourself locked into paying an agency's fees months after you've lost faith in their work.

Month-to-month contracts are ideal, but rare. Most agencies require yearly contracts. Before signing, ask what's involved in canceling the contract if you're not happy with their work. Give extra points to out clauses with minimal hoops, lawyers, and/or termination fees.

What Is the Size of the Agency and Its Amazon Advertising Operation?

This question isn't meant to be a judgment on the number of people working for the agency or whether the agency is owned by a holding company. But you don't want to sign over campaign management to a startup operation. At minimum, the agency should have at least 20 to 30 employees with no less than five analysts dedicated to Amazon Advertising.

The entire agency doesn't need to focus on Amazon, but the Amazon Advertising team definitely should. Is the person building your Amazon campaigns the same person who handles Google Ads or even Amazon listing management? Depth of specialization requires far more than an "Amazon Advertising" bullet point on their website. If you wanted a jack-of-all-trades running your Amazon advertising, you'd be better off crosstraining one of your own employees.

What Additional Services Does the Agency Offer?

If you do 100 percent of your business on Amazon—and see this continuing for at least the next couple of years—then there is no downside to hiring a 100 percent Amazon-focused agency. If, on the other hand, your growth path involves additional paid digital channels, you should give extra points to an agency with a more comprehensive suite of specialization areas.

Specialization is more than meets the eye. Question three may bring this out, but you should steer clear of an opportunistic agency with a thrown-together, incongruent set of shallow service offerings. Even if Amazon advertising is your only current need, ask questions to understand their depth of specialization in other digital channels relevant to your growth. This may involve areas such as paid search advertising through Google, Yahoo!, and Bing; display advertising; conversion-rate optimization; search-engine optimization; and paid social media, such as Facebook, Instagram, and Snapchat.

Why Trust Their Integrity and Expertise?

Trust takes time to build, but the agency selection process typically involves little more than a few phone calls and a couple of presentations. Sure, an agency's integrity and expertise will be much clearer after a few months of working with them, but that won't help you now. You need a shortcut that extends beyond the likability of the salesperson (which, for better or worse, often weighs disproportionately into the final decision).

In the absence of direct experience, trustworthiness is discerned through research and intuition. So, for the best chance of hiring an agency worthy of your trust, review where each stands in relation to the following trust signals:

- Reputable client list, including some role model companies
- Testimonials from clients identified by name
- Thought leadership content and case studies
- Depth and organization of the sales process
- Client reference checks

What Depth and Frequency of Communication Can Be Expected?

Communication defines the quality of all relationships, vendors included. People tend to work with people they know, like, and trust. Everyone has different preferences and expectations when it comes to the style, depth, and frequency of communication with an agency. Some of this is based on your personality, and some is based on the momentum of your business.

Would your job be easier if you could rely on consistently timed reporting updates? Is one agenda-driven scheduled call per month sufficient? Two? Perhaps you're charged with driving 25 to 100 percent year-over-year growth on Amazon; in that case, you may need to meet by phone with your agency team weekly.

Don't read too much into the quality of your interactions with an agency during the sales process—salespeople are financially incentivized to be on-the-ball with responsive and consistent communication! Instead, ask direct questions to understand the level of contact and personal attention provided in typical client relationships. Website testimonials should bear this out. Your expectations should be clearly spelled out in the agreement.

What Structure Is in Place to Ensure Continuity of Client-Specific Expertise?

It's typical for smaller or startup agencies to dedicate a single analyst to each client's account. However, analysts are human: they take vacations, sick days, longer-term leave, or put in their two-week notice because their spouse got a sudden job transfer out of state.

How quickly can the next analyst learn the particulars of your business and brand? Be sure of this: The learning curve is rarely trivial. It takes time to develop an insider understanding of your specific vertical, product line, business goals, operational constraints, brand voice, and campaign structure. This time isn't just the new analyst's, but yours, which you would have already invested bringing the previous analyst up to speed!

Here's the solution: Make sure the agency will assign more than one person to your account. This means that, except for rare occasions, multiple account analysts and/or strategists should participate in *every* agenda-driven call and involve themselves in campaign buildout and optimization. Such a structure is the only way to get the operational redundancy that you're paying for and that an agency should be providing.

What Is Their Investment in Technology?

Amazon's advertising API opens the door to powerful capabilities only accessible to those with the initiative and expertise to engage in custom programming initiatives. Lacking proper resources, most advertisers must content themselves to work exclusively within the capabilities and reporting limitations of Amazon's current web interface.

Proprietary technology not only drives the additional efficiency with which some agencies operate, but intelligent API-powered algorithms and reporting can also confer meaningful competitive advantage to clients.

But be on the lookout for signs that the agency is *too* focused on the strength of their technology. You also need someone at the wheel. As discussed earlier in this chapter, the highest value an agency can provide is *strategic* before it is tactical.

MAKING YOUR FINAL DECISION

The knowledge you've gained in this book gives you the ability to approach agencies with confidence. You know what you're talking about and won't be swayed by sweet-talk or empty promises.

The weight you give each agency's pros and cons is up to you. In the end, your choice will be determined by the answers to your most important questions and the confidence you feel after talking with at least two of their existing clients.

Once you've been relieved of the day-to-day tasks of your Amazon advertising efforts, you can take your thinking up a level. In the next chapter, I'll show you the broader strategy that Amazon lives and breathes by, and it's hidden in plain sight.

Chapter 21

Amazon's Secret Formula for Long-Term Winning

> *Genius . . . is the capacity to see ten things where*
> *the ordinary man sees one.*
>
> —Ezra Pound, American poet (1885–1972)

Assuming strong margins and healthy market demand, business success is really about execution. Execute on the details, and your company will keep pace with the industry.

This is a decent formula for staying in business, but it is not the formula for WINNING.

If you're content with just staying in the race, this may work for you, but if you're like me, you want to win. Winning in business by copying Amazon's core focus is what this chapter is all about.

So who is setting the pace for *your* company?

Competitors are a common pacesetter. It's easy to see the draw—copying their tactics lets you operate without much risk. You'll never win big with this strategy, of course, but you'll almost certainly stay in the race.

Other companies seem to be led by sheer force of will. A firm can sometimes go far through drive and determination, but self-led resolve always hits a wall and deflates. The market will not abide.

In truth, there is only *one* pacesetter with the power to drive you to greatness. It's not your competitors and it's not you. I'm referring, of course, to your customers. (If you're tempted to stop here and think, "Yeah, we do that," please keep reading.)

In this final chapter, let's talk about a winning long-term strategy that will help your business take off on Amazon and beyond. That strategy is all about letting your customers lead.

LET YOUR CUSTOMERS LEAD YOU

If you truly let your customers lead the way, they will transform the race entirely. The competition is no longer about you. Winning becomes an inevitable outcome rather than a forced, top-down mandate.

As I've already mentioned, Amazon is a customer-centered company—and yours should be, too. When a company crosses the $100 billion revenue threshold faster than any other company in history, you can learn from them. Amazon has done a lot of things right, but Jeff Bezos identifies one factor above all others that led to their phenomenal success: *Amazon is led by their customers.* It's reported that Bezos leaves one seat vacant at meetings to keep everyone aware of the silent participant who should have the loudest voice in the room.

In order to **do** what's best for your customers, you need to **know** what's best for them.

Amazon only knows what's best for their customers because Amazon listens intently to them. The resulting understanding affects more than marketing messages and product selection. The core of Amazon's business operations is molded in direct response to what their customers want.

In 2013, for example, when UPS overpromised and underdelivered, mostly for Amazon's air shipments due by Christmas Eve, Amazon benefited from UPS's PR nightmare by proactively issuing $20 gift cards for any Amazon customer who didn't get their order in time for Christmas even if they had delivered the product to UPS on time.

There's much you can learn about how Amazon does business. And just because they're the 800-pound gorilla of ecommerce today doesn't mean they'll always be that dominant in the future. Just like Walmart founder Sam Walton patiently learned from the retail kings of his early days (Sears and Kmart), you too can learn from Jeff Bezos.

Humans are creatures of emotion. When it comes to making purchases, once we decide what we want, we usually want it NOW. Bezos recognizes that and has been aggressively leading the charge to shorten the window from "you want it" to "you've got it."

Ecommerce has its roots in the catalog business, but Bezos has worked extremely hard to change the assumptions built into a model where you get what you want without going to a store. The need for speed has never been more acute.

FASTER, FASTER, FASTER!

Free delivery. Two-day delivery. Next-day delivery. Same-day delivery. Two-hour delivery.

It's a never-ending journey because customers will always want fast delivery and low prices, and they will always want to be delighted by your products.

To work toward those customer-focused objectives, Amazon has spent billions building a complex web of warehouse, distribution, and sortation centers—often bypassing short-term profits to do so.

When it comes to delivery speed, I love what Bezos says here:

It's impossible to imagine a future ten years from now where a customer comes up and says, "Jeff, I love Amazon; I just wish the prices were a little higher," [or] "I love Amazon; I just wish you'd deliver a little more slowly." Impossible. And so the effort we put into those things, spinning those things up, we know the energy we put into it today will still be paying off dividends for our customers ten years from now. When you have something that you know is true, even over the long term, you can afford to put a lot of energy into it.

Here's an example of Bezos' idea in action. Two years ago on a warm spring Sunday morning, I was at home outlining a speech on entrepreneurship I was slated to give to a group of business-school students, when I realized I needed a specific book—and I needed it *now*. After checking the Barnes & Noble website to see if the book was in stock at any of the local stores (it wasn't), I remembered Amazon's Prime Now app. I was astonished to find a single copy of the exact book I needed in stock, thanks to Amazon having and using data that their land-bound competitor ignored.

Further investigation revealed that a month prior, Amazon had opened a 40,000-square-foot warehouse in Raleigh, just nine miles from my home, with delivery for its Prime members free within a two-hour window.

I put the book into my shopping cart and discovered I was short of their $20 minimum. Some bottled water and yogurt did the trick. At the last minute, I decided to upgrade to one-hour delivery for an additional $7.99. The smiling delivery driver arrived at my doorstep 32 minutes later with my order (shown in Figure 21–1 on page 194). Faster, faster, faster was the promise, and Amazon delivered.

FIGURE 21–1. Delivered Amazon Prime Now Order

WHY NOT JUST SAY YES?

People tend to see their firm's operational limitations as an immovable baseline. But when you begin buying your own airplanes so you can get packages to your customers faster and cheaper than you can with FedEx, you're operating in the world dreamed up by your customers.

While everyone else says matter-of-factly, "No, I'm sorry, we can't do that," winning firms are inspired by their customers' dreams and vow to create this new reality for themselves and their customers to enjoy.

Amazon can continue to make these operational investments because it's a Goliath for whom money is no object. You will probably have to be more selective. Or you can choose to piggyback on Amazon's supply chain structures to complement your own demand and operational infrastructure.

To fulfill demand and ensure speedy delivery, Amazon's operational infrastructure boasts more than 75 fulfillment centers and 25 sortation centers across North America and employs more than 125,000 full-time hourly employees plus 100,000 seasonal workers in the U.S. alone. Half the U.S. population now lives within 20 miles of an Amazon warehouse. It's up to you to determine if and how you want to leverage their supply chain and advertising platform.

Your ability to say "yes" to customers' questions or desires that play perfectly into your brand's strengths will help determine your business' success.

Touching the
Future of Retail

*The future belongs to those who believe in the
beauty of their dreams.*

—UNKNOWN

The year 2017 saw more U.S. retail store closings than any other year in history. But don't misinterpret this fact. Sure, poorly integrated retail stores may be going away, but it would be a mistake to write off physical retail altogether.

There's a reason Amazon paid $13.7 billion to acquire the grocery store chain Whole Foods in August 2017 (see Figure E–1 on page 198).

In this section, I'll talk about the future of retail and how to leverage it for your brand.

Though not growing nearly as fast as ecommerce (4.4 percent vs. 16 percent in 2017), in-person retail nevertheless continues to gain ground.

Ecommerce solves the long tail product distribution and convenience problem, but for a shopping experience, nothing touches a physical presence. Ironically, brick-and-mortar is becoming digital's strongest differentiator.

FIGURE E-1. Whole Foods

Ecommerce upstart Warby Parker has nearly 100 retail locations, which account for more than half of their overall sales volume. They don't care if you visit a retail location to try on their eyeglasses. In fact, they encourage it. They make money either way.

To pull this off, you need to formulate your distribution and retail strategies around this reality. Ecommerce optimizes for convenience and cost, but humans are optimized for physical experiences. Retailers setting themselves up for future success are marrying experience with ecommerce.

You can spend your energy trying to persuade customers to buy through your most profitable channel, or you can focus on making profitable sales wherever customers are already searching and buying.

Swim with today's current, not yesterday's. Your choice becomes easier when you consider that today's customers are preconditioned to finish the checkout process without the product in hand. Physical stores don't need to carry your entire line of inventory—or much inventory at all.

Here are a few ways progressive retailers are embracing retail experiences:

- As an advertising channel for your brand's ecommerce store
- As a campaign engagement testing venue for your brand
- As an affiliate marketing channel via in-store kiosks

Where is your physical/digital strategy headed?

HOW TO GROW: THE CORE FOUR FOR COMMERCE

To close this book, I'd like to take a moment to reflect on how you, as a brand professional, can grow both on Amazon and beyond. To me, there really are four core tenets for commerce that broadly apply, no matter what your brand sells. If you can hang tightly to these core four concepts, I have no doubt you will succeed.

My own management philosophy is to focus my time and energy on the vital few and delegate the trivial many.

What are the vital few in commerce? Here are four you should focus on to ensure your company never plateaus or gets stuck in a rut: marketing, human capital, inventory, and space and equipment.

Marketing

"Nothing happens until somebody sells something." You've likely heard that a dozen times. But in the world of consumer commerce, you can't sell anything until marketing happens.

According to a 2017 study of 2,000 U.S. consumers by ad and market research firm Survata, 85 percent of consumers began their product search on either Amazon (49 percent) or a traditional search engine such as Google (36 percent). Although Amazon and search together drive the highest portion of discovery online, don't rely on these two channels alone.

Keep growing by upgrading your website and adding awesome content (compelling descriptions, detailed pictures, videos, etc.) to increase your conversion rates on both amazon and your own website, and keep in touch with your customers through smart, segmented email offers. Test broad media channels such as radio, television, and digital display. If you sell direct to consumers, test a series of print catalogs targeted to existing customers.

Human Capital

John Paul DeJoria could never have grown the way he did if he had simply kept selling shampoo door-to-door with partner Paul Mitchell. Today DeJoria employs thousands of people in his far-flung enterprises, helping himself and others in his community grow. You can do the same.

Inventory

There's a saying in retail: "You can't sell from an empty wagon." I repeatedly found this to be true in my former retail/wholesale company. I'd add several new or expanded product lines and/or SKUs, and within weeks our sales and profits would go up. Our most successful clients (those who grow strongly year after year) do this as consistently as breathing. Amazon is constantly adding depth and breadth to their product lines, both through deliberate product line extension (they entered the office equipment and industrial supplies business, Amazon Business, in 2015, for example) and through increased coverage via their marketplace.

Space and Equipment

To grow, you have to keep pushing the envelope when it comes to space and equipment. If you have "just enough space" in your office or warehouse, you will likely plateau your business. With "just enough space," you cannot invest in additional product lines, hire more staff, or take advantage of occasional truckload deals on product or raw materials.

One of our clients has consistently grown by 60 to 100 percent each year for a decade by upgrading his warehouse by three to four times with each move. On his fourth and most recent move, he bought his own warehouse and is focused on paying off the mortgage before he needs to move again. That's a smart way to build a robust commercial real estate portfolio along the way, too.

Here at ROI, we're constantly adding new laptops, servers, monitors, chairs, desks, and software. Perhaps you're investing in new pallet racks, lift trucks, or a new conveyor system for your warehouse.

To keep growing, continue to press the envelope on the core four. If you do that, you will see your brand grow, thrive, and prosper for years to come. Happy advertising!

Glossary

Advertising Cost of Sales (ACoS): The ratio of direct advertising spend to the sales directly triggered by that spend (ACoS = Ad Spend ÷ Sales).

Amazon Demand-Side Platform (DSP): A demand-side platform that enables advertisers to programmatically reach Amazon and Advertiser audiences on Amazon sites and apps, across the web, and on devices.

Amazon Standard Identification Number (ASIN): Unique blocks of 10 letters and/or numbers that identify products for sale on Amazon. For books, the ASIN is the same as the ISBN, but for all other products a new ASIN is created when an item is uploaded to the Amazon catalog. ASINs are found on the product detail page.

Average Order Value (AOV): The ratio of total revenue by the number of orders (AOV = Total Revenue ÷ Total Number of Orders).

Brand Keywords: Keywords that target your specific brand and products.

Buy Box: The white box that appears on the right side of the Amazon product detail page, where customers can add the item they are viewing for purchase to their shopping cart.

Category/Nonbranded Keywords: Keywords that are not associated with a specific brand name but rather with target category-level keyword traffic. This is sometimes referred to as "nonbranded" or "brand awareness."

Clickthrough Rate (CTR): The total number of clicks on an ad divided by the total number of impressions, expressed as a percentage.

Competitor Keywords: Keywords that target your competitors' products and brand.

Conversion Rate Optimization (CRO): A branch of digital marketing that aims to improve the conversion rate of web pages through A/B split testing, thus making the pages more profitable.

Cost Per Acquisition (CPA): A pricing model in which companies are charged by advertising platforms only when leads, sales, or conversions are generated.

Cost Per Click (CPC): The price of a click made on an ad that leads people to a specified product page or website.

Enhanced Brand Content (EBC): An Amazon feature that enables registered brand owners to change the product descriptions of brand ASINs. Adding EBC to your product detail pages can result in higher conversion rates, increased traffic, and increased sales when used effectively.

European Article Number (EAN): A 12- or 13-digit product identification code used throughout Europe that uniquely identifies the product, manufacturer, and its attributes. An EAN is typically printed on a product label or packaging as a bar code.

Fulfillment by Amazon (FBA): A program through Amazon in which a company stores their products in Amazon's fulfillment centers, and they pick, pack, ship, and provide customer service for those products.

International Standard Book Number (ISBN): A unique commercial book identifier bar code composed of either 10 or 13 digits, typically printed on the back cover of a book.

Key Performance Indicator (KPI): A measurable numerical indicator (typically) used by marketers and business executives to track the most important numbers against their goals, including but not limited to revenue, conversion rate, total ad costs, and total payroll.

Minimum Advertised Price (MAP): A number set by brand owners that mandates the lowest price for which a retailer can advertise a specific product in online or print ads.

Pay-Per-Click (PPC): A form of advertising in which advertisers pay only when a user clicks on an ad or link (vs. paying per display or action).

Product Display Ad: A self-service display ad for individual ASINs that allows brands to target behavioral segments or relevant products. These ads show on product detail pages to display either complementary or competing products.

Return on Ad Spend (ROAS): A digital marketing metric that demonstrates the profit made, as compared to the amount of money spent on the ads.

Seller Central: The Amazon web interface used by brands and merchants to market and sell their products directly to Amazon's customers. If you have a Seller Central account, you're considered a marketplace or third-party seller.

Sponsored Brands: Keyword-targeted banner ads that promote products throughout the search results page.

Sponsored Products: Keyword-targeted ads that enable you to promote the products you sell in highly visible placements on Amazon.com's search results page.

Stock Keeping Unit (SKU): Product and service identification code for a store or product, often displayed as a machine-readable bar code that helps track the item for inventory.

Total Advertising Cost of Sales (TACoS): A metric that contextualizes your ad spend at a much higher level and can bring clarity on where the hard limits for your ad spend are even in the most aggressive growth plays.

Universal Product Code (UPC): A 12-digit bar code used extensively on retail packaging in the United States.

Vendor Central: The Amazon web interface used by manufacturers and distributors. If you sell via Vendor Central, you're called a first-party seller. You're acting as a supplier, selling in bulk to Amazon. Registration on Vendor Central is by invitation only.

Acknowledgments

Any big project takes the dedicated effort of a true team. Without these rock stars, this book wouldn't have been possible. I'm incredibly grateful to Ben Smith and Grayson Cross for contributing the bulk of the "how to" portion; to Alyona DelaCoeur for formulating the original outline and proposal; to Chris Crompton for his contribution to the business insights and color as well as the bulk of the agency chapter; to Emma Anderson, our grammar and style guide expert for keeping us grammatically correct, super organized, and on point; to Megan Ingros for organizing and cataloging our client stories; to Joseph Arcos for generously loaning us his solid editorial and storytelling expertise; to Tanner McCaskey for gifting us his unique graphics arts talents through the book's illustrations; to my assistant Dana Hedman for keeping the team scheduled and fed and my own calendar free; to Jennifer Dorsey (editorial director at Entrepreneur Press®) for her edits and countless "flesh this out more" asks; to Mike Ewasyshyn, Andrew Reagan, Taylor Moore, Phuong Le, David Stone, and Mallory Bartles for their numerous technical contributions; and finally, to my dear friend Perry Marshall for recommending me to the team at Entrepreneur Press®.

About the Author

Timothy leads ROI Revolution in its mission to drive growth for brands, retailers, and ecommerce merchants with its results-driven digital-marketing technology and services. Timothy founded the company in June 2002. With his extensive marketing and retail background, he is a thought leader who has spoken at 70+ industry, ecommerce, and Amazon focused events including IRCE, the world's largest ecommerce conference. He is a guest lecturer at North Carolina State University's Poole College of Management and has contributed to key industry publications, including *Internet Retailer*.

Timothy is a *summa cum laude* graduate of Florida Gulf Coast University (2001) with a bachelor's degree in Computer Science.

Timothy would truly appreciate your feedback and would love to hear what you have to say about the book. Connect with him on LinkedIn at https://www.linkedin.com/in/timothyseward.

Thank You for Purchasing the
Ultimate Guide to Amazon Advertising!

Claim your access to **book updates** and **bonus content** designed to fast-track your brand's growth on Amazon.

What you'll get:

- Updates on the ever-changing landscape of Amazon advertising.

- New Amazon strategy reports for brand marketing executives, including *Amazon Advertising for Brands* and *Amazon Stores + Sponsored Brands: Taming the Two-Headed Monster*.

- Instant access to **Amazon strategy training videos** covering a range of topics such as the latest ad formats, fulfillment options, and steps to defend your brand's product pages.

- *Scientific Advertising* by Claude Hopkins.

- A compilation of links and resources to the top tools available to help streamline and optimize your brand's presence on Amazon.

 Go to roirevolution.com/amazonadvertising to access your up-to-date bonus content.

Index